TWAYNE'S WORLD AUTHORS SERIES

A Survey of the World's Literature

SPAIN

Janet W. Diaz, Texas Tech University

EDITOR

Víctor Ruiz Iriarte

TWAS 540

VÍCTOR RUIZ IRIARTE

By Phyllis Zatlin Boring

Rutgers University

TWAYNE PUBLISHERS

A DIVISION OF G. K. HALL & CO., BOSTON

Published in 1980 by Twayne Publishers,
A Division of G. K. Hall & Co.
All Rights Reserved

Printed on permanent/durable acid-free paper and bound
in the United States of America

First Printing

Frontispiece photograph of Víctor Ruiz Iriarte.

Library of Congress Cataloging in Publication Data

Boring, Phyllis Zatlin.
Víctor Ruiz Iriarte.

(Twayne's world authors series; TWAS 540: Spain)
Bibliography: Pp. 140–45
Includes index.
1.   Ruiz Iriarte, Víctor—Criticism and interpretation.
PQ6633.U52Z58   862'.6'4   79-4595
ISBN 0-8057-6382-1

Contents

About the Author

Preface

Chronology

1. Víctor Ruiz Iriarte: Man of the Theater   13

2. Life As Theater: The World of Poetic Fantasy   27

3. The Satirical Farces   45

4. Role Playing and Role Reversal:
   The Comedies of Manners   52

5. Theater As Fun   75

6. The Serious Dramas   83

7. The Television Plays   102

8. The Later Comedies   113

9. Conclusion   124

Notes and References   127

Selected Bibliography   140

Index   146

About the Author

Phyllis Zatlin Boring holds the A. B. in Spanish and French from Rollins College (Winter Park, Florida) and the M. A. and Ph. D. in Romance Languages from the University of Florida. She presently is Associate Professor of Spanish and Portuguese and Associate Dean at Rutgers College of Rutgers University (New Jersey). Her primary scholarly interest is the contemporary Spanish novel and theater, and she has published articles in various journals including *Romance Notes, Modern Drama, Kentucky Romance Quarterly, Papers on Language & Literature, CLA Journal, Estreno, Comparative Literature Studies, Hispanófila, Foreign Language Annals, Luso-Brazilian Review,* and *Revista de Estudios Hispánicos.* She is co-author of an intermediate level Spanish textbook *Lengua y lectura,* editor of a college edition of Francisco Ayala's novel *El rapto,* and author of the study *Elena Quiroga* in the Twayne World Authors Series.

Preface

One of the first new playwrights to appear in the Spanish theater in the years immediately following the Civil War, Víctor Ruiz Iriarte has had a long and distinguished career as an author of dramatic works, primarily comedies. His plays have received a number of important awards, including the Piquer Prize of the Royal Spanish Academy, the National Theater Prize, the National Literature Prize, and the María Rolland Prize. Additionally, his series of television plays has been awarded the National Television Prize. An extremely active figure in the theatrical and literary world of Madrid, Ruiz Iriarte has, in addition to his plays for both television and the stage, collaborated on movie scripts, directed his own plays, and written numerous articles over a forty-year period for major Spanish newspapers and literary journals. In recognition of his leadership in the field, he has been chosen to serve as president of the Association of Spanish Authors and of the Spanish Authors' Pension Fund. Ruiz Iriarte's plays have been staged throughout Spain, Europe, and Latin America. In the United States there are student editions available of three of his full-length plays as well as a collection of his television plays. There are, however, no published translations in English of any of his works and the only book-length study available on his theater is in Spanish. Even that study does not represent a comprehensive, critical analysis of Ruiz Iriarte's complete theatrical works to date. The present book is intended to provide such an analysis.

In the 1940s and 1950s, official censorship in Spain, coupled with the prevailing attitude of the theater-going public, encouraged light comedy over serious drama. The majority of Ruiz Iriarte's plays fell within the range of comedy then in favor. He emphasized works of poetic fantasy and comedies of manners, along with an occasional light satire. Although critics who felt that the stage should be concentrating on the real problems of contemporary society rejected his comedies and farces as frivolous, these early works of Ruiz Iriarte include several important successes that are well written, well constructed, and perhaps more universal in their appeal than some of the

Spanish plays of social protest that began to appear in the late 1950s. Unquestionably Ruiz Iriarte developed his own style and stamp of individuality in these comedies which, in their own way, form a document reflecting the changing values of the Spanish middle class in the postwar years. In the 1960s, following a relaxation of censorship, Ruiz Iriarte produced two serious dramas which in particular demonstrated his versatility as a playwright and his deep concern with human problems. In spite of these triumphs, he continues to consider himself primarily a writer of comedies, a form of theater which he vigorously defends, and his most recent works fall within the subgenre.

For the purpose of analyzing Ruiz Iriarte's extensive theater, I have divided the plays into several groups: poetic fantasy, satire, comedies of manners, theatrical games, serious drama, and the later comedies. I have chosen this division primarily by subgenre in preference to a more chronological organization because the latter would have allowed less comparison of related works. Omitted from the discussions are a few plays that have remained unpublished. The author himself decided that certain of his works should be consigned to oblivion and those manuscripts are no longer accessible. In the early 1940s, when his plays were first staged, he similarly destroyed all of his earlier efforts at writing theater. In approaching his published plays, I have attempted to identify major recurrent themes, characters and techniques, as well as to point out relationships between the works of Ruiz Iriarte and those of other Spanish and European playwrights. Additionally, there is a chapter devoted to his published television plays. I have excluded from the present study his work with motion pictures in that his scriptwriting has generally consisted of collaborations and adaptations rather than original plays. Although I make occasional references to his essays and articles where they relate to his theater, I have not included a special analysis of his newspaper writings. Ruiz Iriarte's journalistic career has been very long, and his essays on a variety of topics have been published in divers newspapers and journals, some of them now very difficult to locate. More importantly, however, they fall outside the literary focus of the present study.

In the preparation of the present study I have been fortunate in having the full and generous cooperation of Víctor Ruiz Iriarte, who patiently answered my many questions, sometimes even taking the time to prepare written statements on some of the issues I raised. I am particularly grateful to him for providing biographical data that would otherwise not have been available and copies of his writings that otherwise would have been difficult to secure. I am very much indebted to the playwright for his cooperation with my research and also personally appreciative of the kindness and courtesy he extended to my children and me during our visits to Spain. I would also like to thank Professor Janet Winecoff Díaz for her enthusiasm and encouragement throughout this project and Professor Marion P. Holt for his helpful suggestions at the beginning of my research. I am grateful, as always, to Doris Caruso and Linda Puzzelento for their careful and thoughtful assistance in the preparation of the manuscript; to Barbara Carballal, for her willingness to share with me her knowledge of the theater in Madrid; and to the Rutgers University Research Council, for their material support of this project.

PHYLLIS ZATLIN BORING

Rutgers University

Chronology

1912   April 24: Víctor Ruiz Iriarte born in Madrid.
1922   Enters the Colegio de los Hermanos Maristas to prepare *bachillerato* (high school diploma).
1931   Begins writing for various newspapers.
1936–   Spanish Civil War. Complete interruption of literary career.
1939
1940   Joins group of young writers at the Café de Gijón. Begins collaboration in several literary journals, including *Garcilaso*, *La Estafeta Literaria*, *El Español*, and *Fantasía*.
1943   September 23: university group in Zaragoza stages one-act play, *Un día en la gloria* [A day in glory].
1945   February 6: première in Madrid of *El puente de los suicidas* [Suicide bridge] at the Reina Victoria Theater.
1946   Wins Piquer Prize of the Royal Academy for *Academia de amor* [Academy of love].
1949   April 16: première in Madrid at the Infanta Isabel Theater of *El aprendiz de amante* [The apprentice lover], first commercial success.
1950   Embarks on career as movie scriptwriter, and becomes regular contributor to two important newspapers, *Informaciones* (Madrid) and *El Noticiero Universal* (Barcelona). May 26: première of *El landó de seis caballos* [The six-horse landau] at the María Guerrero Theater. December 8: première of *El gran minué* [The grand minuet] at the Teatro Español.
1952   Wins National Theater Prize for *Juego de niños* [Child's play].
1953   April 4: Opening at the Teatro Comíco of *El pobrecito embustero* [The poor little liar].
1955   November 18: *La guerra empieza en Cuba* [The war begins in Cuba] opens in the Reina Victoria Theater.
1958   December 12: opening of *Esta noche es la víspera* [Tonight is the prelude] at the Goya Theater.
1962   Publication of *Un pequeño mundo* [A small world], a collection of newspaper articles.

1964   December 4: première of *El carrusell* [The carousel] at the Lara Theater.

1965   Begins writing plays for television. September 14: *Un paraguas bajo la lluvia* [An umbrella under the rain] opens at the Teatro de la Comedia.

1966   Wins National Television Prize for *La pequeña comedia* [Little theater], a series of television plays.

1967   Wins National Literature Prize for *La muchacha del sombrerito rosa* [The girl in the little pink hat]. September 15: *La señora recibe una carta* [The lady receives a letter] opens at the Teatro de la Comedia.

1969   Wins María Rolland Prize for *Primavera en la Plaza de París* [Springtime in the Plaza de París]. February 27: *Historia de un adulterio* [Story of Adultery] opens in Valle-Inclán Theater. Elected president of Sociedad General de Autores de España (Association of Spanish Authors).

1975   September 25: *Buenas noches, Sabina* [Good evening, Sabina] opens in Arlequín Theater. Begins writing syndicated column for distribution by EFE in addition to regular contributions to the Madrid newspaper *ABC*.

1977   Begins service as president of Montepío de Autores Españoles (Spanish Authors' Pension Fund).

CHAPTER 1

Víctor Ruiz Iriarte:
Man of the Theater

I The Making of a Playwright

VÍCTOR Ruiz Iriarte was born in Madrid on April 24, 1912, the oldest of four children of Víctor Ruiz Fraguas and Emilia Iriarte Sanz.[1] His father was from Zaragoza and his mother was also born in Aragón, but Ruiz Iriarte's ties are definitely to the Spanish capital where he has lived all his life. His early years were in many ways typical for a Spanish child of a middle-class city family of the period. In his newspaper and magazine articles he has written on occasion of the children of his time and their common experiences: the adventure of a train trip to San Sebastián for summer vacation; the sailor suits little boys wore when they dressed up; family strolls in the Plaza Mayor; Thursday afternoons at Charlie Chaplin or Tom Mix movies; an occasional trip to the theater to see the great actress María Guerrero or a play by Galdós. As an adult, Ruiz Iriarte in his writings has successfully evoked the Madrid of his childhood, but he doubts that he was a happy child. Childhood, he explains, is a stage of our lives that keeps its own secrets and which we can never really recapture (*T* 1:44).

Ruiz Iriarte nevertheless does remember that his first creative inclination was not to the theater but to drawing. He dreamed of becoming a great painter and drew sketches of the friends who came to visit his parents. Like other Spanish boys, he was also attracted to bullfighting and soccer and amused his three younger sisters, Pilar, María Luisa, and María Francisca, by practicing with his cape or kicking the ball in the house (*T* 2:43). Although he did not actually try writing plays until he was fifteen, his contact with theater began earlier. His father, who for a time was very interested in drama, belonged to an amateur theatrical group. When Víctor and Pilar were still quite small, the group planned a benefit performance of *La sobrina de cura* [The priest's niece] by Arniches, a play whose cast called for several poor children. Ruiz Fraguas offered the services of his son and daughter, but their mother was unwilling to have them appear in public dressed in anything less than their best clothes. Ruiz Iriarte humorously recalls that his theatrical debut was not a brilliant success: "It's painful to confess, but I almost cried" (T 1:45).

Like many other children, little Víctor also had a puppet theater. With the stage set up on the dining room table, he would make up plays for his sisters, who proved to be a polite but indifferent audience and rebelled when he tried to make them pay admission. His histrionic talents then took the form of imitations of other people, which he performed in front of a mirror. "Perhaps a psychologist would see the first indications of a theatrical vocation" in those imitations, he suggests, for "every author carries within himself, as a constituent of his personality, a large segment of comic actor" (T 2:42).

When he was ten, Víctor was sent to the Colegio de los Hermanos Maristas, a parochial school located on the Paseo del Cisne, where he was to prepare his *bachillerato* (high school diploma). He found as a student that he disliked mathematics but enjoyed history and literature. At home he discovered his father's collection of "La Novela Teatral" (The Theatrical Novel) and became an avid reader of plays by Rusiñol, García Álvarez, Casero, Villaespesa, Arniches, Benavente and others. He was fascinated by the comedies, learning passages by heart, and lost interest in the adventure novels he had previously read. The characters in the plays had a seductive charm for him: "These indeed were marvelous beings who could make one laugh or cry. It was the Great Miracle. It was Theater" (T 2:44). He began to buy his own plays at second hand book stalls and followed the play reviews in the newspaper. It was at this high pitch of enthusiasm, and inspired by the *sainetes* (popular farces) of Arniches, Casero, and García Álvarez, that Ruiz Iriarte wrote his first comedy. He read the play to his family. His father laughed and his mother felt that it was much better than many comedies she had seen in Madrid. His sisters, on the other hand, became very gloomy, fearing the worst for their brother's future.

Convinced then as now that his true vocation was writing plays, Ruiz Iriarte continued to create dramas and comedies. Like other beginning authors, he found himself working in uncertainty and solitude. But, he believes, there is no way to teach someone to write plays: "Theater can have no university; it is rigorously self-taught" (T 2:46). The playwright must be his own student and his own master.

From his later perspective as a successful writer of comedies, Ruiz Iriarte has frequently noted that the true playwright considers theater a craft and learns the techniques of the trade. He must understand the importance of dialogue, of situation, of actors, and of audience to create a theatrical work.[2] The result is worth the effort. For Ruiz Iriarte theater is "magic, witchcraft, charm, fascination." [3] "I love the theater. I firmly believe that theater is one of the fundamental accomplishments that have blossomed from the human spirit." [4]

Ruiz Iriarte's love for the theater and his sense that this was indeed his calling were not extinguished in spite of more than ten years of unsuccessful efforts at having his plays staged. In the early 1930s, following his graduation from high school, he began to make the rounds of theaters, hoping that an important actor, actress, or director would at least consider his scripts. He recalls those years of failure not only without bitterness but even with humor. The theater world was impenetrable for young writers who could not even get past the doorman: "You stood looking at the ugly face of that omnipotent being, your thoughts filled with conflicting ideas, all of them sinister. But resistance was useless. As you walked away you could hear the doorman comment, 'Another one!' " (*T* 2:45). Although Ruiz Iriarte did not let this early discouragement deter him from pursuing his goal, his failure as an apprentice playwright did take an emotional toll: "I, being a timid boy who had a difficult time socializing, remember melancholy as the dominant characteristic of my early youth" (*T* 3:41).[5] When he was refused interviews by newspaper directors, or when theatrical producers rejected his plays without reading them, he would take long walks through the city and seek refuge in his own thoughts.

Finding the doors of the Madrid theaters closed to him, Ruiz Iriarte decided to make a name for himself as a journalist. His first article was published in 1931 and dealt with women orators. It was inspired by a political speech he heard in the street one day in the Chamberí district. His next two articles were also of a political nature, commenting on Alejandro Lerroux and Adolf Hitler. Ruiz Iriarte observes that both Lerroux and Hitler ignored his advice (*T* 3:38). These first efforts were followed by regular contributions to *Ciudad*, a newspaper founded and directed by Víctor de la Serna, son of the novelist Concha Espina. Espina at that time was paid fifty *pesetas* per article; Ruiz Iriarte was pleased to get twenty.

A friend introduced the young writer to Pedro Mourlane Michelena, an editor of *El Sol*, and Ruiz Iriarte was given the opportunity to write book reviews—without pay. The reviews were published with only initials at the bottom, a practice that distressed the would-be playwright: "As the principal motive for my entering journalism was to become famous as fast as possible so that the theater doormen would not keep me from going in, I decided to change this custom and sign my work with my full name" (T 3:39). The try failed, however, as the name was always changed back to initials. Enrique Mullor, editor of a weekly for which Ruiz Iriarte also wrote, assured him that he, too, had started out hoping to be a playwright but that neither of them would ever see their plays staged.

This journalistic career, while it did not prove to be a quick route to success as a playwright as Ruiz Iriarte had hoped, did benefit him in an unsuspected way. He began to write with more precision and to seek a concise style. With pencil in hand, he would strike from each article all unnecessary words, carefully editing the piece before submitting it for publication. If a light newspaper essay required such attention, what would a play require? How many scenes could be omitted? How many dialogues could be shortened? "It is clear that, with respect to time and language, theater, the technique of theatrical construction, is not a problem of extension but of concision. Theater is pure synthesis, pure suggestion" (T 3:40).

In 1936, with the outbreak of the Spanish Civil War, Ruiz Iriarte's fledgling journalistic career was interrupted. The war years represent a total break in his literary activity. In the early 1940s, however, he not only returned to his efforts but finally established himself both as an essayist and a playwright. He became part of a group of young writers and artists who met at the Café de Gijón. From that group, known as the "Juventud Creadora" ("Creative Youth"), there emerged one famous novelist, Camilo José Cela, and one famous playwright, Ruiz Iriarte. Before either of these two writers had published in the genres for which they were to become known, they agreed to dedicate works to one another (T 6:30). Cela's first novel La familia de Pascual Duarte [The family of Pascual Duarte, 1942] is thus dedicated to Ruiz Iriarte and the playwright, in turn, dedicated his El puente de los suicidas [Suicide bridge] to Cela. From this period also dates Ruiz Iriarte's collaboration in important literary magazines of the day: Garcilaso, La Estafeta Literaria, El Español, and Fantasía. Finally, in 1943, his one-act play Un día en la gloria [A day in glory] was presented by a university troupe in Zaragoza, and the following year a professional company staged Suicide Bridge in San Sebastián.

The staging of A Day in Glory came to Ruiz Iriarte as a complete surprise. The play had been published in a journal and the group in Zaragoza prepared the production without contacting the author. "My first première, after ten years of trying in vain, was . . . by coincidence and without my knowledge." [6] To María Arias, who decided to produce *Suicide Bridge* in the provinces, he attributes unbelievable generosity, for "new authors were never staged, no matter what happened." He similarly remembers with gratitude the affection and enthusiasm that Tina Gascó and Fernando Granada displayed toward the same play. It was their troupe which gave Ruiz Iriarte his first première in Madrid. They continued to collaborate with him on several of his important early plays. Having at last reached his goal, the playwright destroyed eighteen plays that he had written before *Suicide Bridge* and *A Day in Glory* and proceeded to write new comedies.

II An Active Career

From the early 1940s until the present, Ruiz Iriarte has remained actively involved in the entertainment world of Spain, not only in the theater as both writer and director but also later as a scriptwriter for motion pictures and television. His contribution to newspapers and magazines has also continued throughout his career. In many respects his life has revolved around his work. "My private life, as you will see, is of little interest," he once told an interviewer. "Basically I'm a solitary person." [7] The pastimes he mentions are all related to his vocation: going to the theater and movies, visiting with friends who are similarly interested in theater and literature. A bachelor, he currently lives in an apartment near the Glorieta de Quevedo in the Chamberí district where he has spent most of his life. His sister María Luisa lives with him. Pilar is a nun, residing in Mexico, and the youngest sister, María Francisca is married and lives with her family in Valencia. Their mother, now in her nineties, makes her home with María Francisca. Their father died in 1951. For a number of years, Ruiz Iriarte owned a summer retreat in El Escorial and has traveled throughout Spain as well as to Argentina, France, Italy, Portugal, and Switzerland. Although some trips have been related to productions of his own plays, he believes that the only ones that may have had an impact on his writing have been those to Paris.

The première in Madrid in 1945 of *Suicide Bridge* was more of a critical success than a commercial one. This was not enough to establish Ruiz Iriarte as one of the important new playwrights of the postwar period. A second play, also starring Tina Gascó, opened in Madrid that same year, *Don Juan se ha puesto triste* [Don Juan has become sad] but has never been published; it is one of several plays which although staged at one time the author has since condemned to oblivion. With his third professional production in Madrid, *Academia de amor* [Academy of love], Ruiz Iriarte won the Piquer prize of the Royal Academy for 1946. This achievement was followed by two comedies in 1947, *El cielo está cerca*, [Heaven is near] and *La señora, sus ángeles y el diablo* [The lady, her angels, and the Devil], neither of which has been published and the first of which the playwright has labeled his "greatest failure." [8] In 1949, with the opening in Madrid of *El aprendiz de amante* [The apprentice lover], starring Carmen Carbonell and Antonio Vico, Ruiz Iriarte obtained his first important commercial success and earned a place of prominence in the contemporary Spanish theater. The same year *Las mujeres decentes* [Respectable women] was produced in both Barcelona and Madrid, and in 1950 the Madrid productions of two important plays, *El landó de seis caballos* [The six-horse landau] and *El gran minué* [The grand minuet], reinforced his growing reputation as a writer of comedies.

The plays of the 1940s were varied not only in their success but in their themes and intent. The period included, besides the comedies and farces already mentioned, two serious dramas, the unpublished *Los pájaros ciegos* [Blind birds, 1948] and the one-act experimental piece *Juanita va a Rio de Janeiro* [Juanita goes to Rio de Janeiro, 1948].

Among these early plays one can find both the major and minor tendencies of Ruiz Iriarte's later theater. *Suicide Bridge* introduced a series of comedies of poetic fantasy, plays in which the characters themselves create large-scale illusions in order to escape or help others escape from reality. These reflect some influence of Alejandro Casona and Luigi Pirandello and, even more importantly, Nikolai Evreinov. *The Apprentice Lover*, which may be classified as a comedy of manners for its portrayal of the customs of contemporary Spanish society, established a pattern which dominated Ruiz Iriarte's plays of the 1950s: mildly satirical works in which one or more characters assumed false roles in order to win the love of their spouses or achieve some other goal. With *The Grand Minuet* Ruiz Iriarte moved to a historical setting and emphasized satire, as he had earlier done in *A Day in Glory*. Serious drama, announced in *Blind Birds*, reappeared ten years later and accounted for two of his important triumphs of the 1960s.

The 1950s was a period of great productivity for Ruiz Iriarte, perhaps in part because his comedies of manners were based on a recurrent pattern. From 1951 to 1960, he had fourteen plays open in Madrid or Barcelona. Of the several that fall into the category of comedy of manners, the most notable was *Juego de niños* [Child's play], winner of The National Theater Prize for 1952, which starred Tina Gascó and was dedicated to her. Gascó created the leading role in four other plays of the decade while Carmen Carbonell and Antonio Vico starred in two of them. Although the comedies of manners predominated, Ruiz Iriarte also wrote one more play which may be classified as poetic fantasy, another satire, a farce with an historical setting, and, in 1958, a serious drama, *Esta noche es la víspera* [Tonight is the prelude]. In general the comedies of this decade, though box office hits, were often viewed negatively by some critics who found them too frivolous. Three of these plays have been judged failures by the author himself and have remained unpublished: *También la buena gente* [Good people, too, 1957], *Una investigación privada* [A private investigation, 1958], and *De París viene mamá* [Mama's coming from Paris, 1960].

Even if the comedies of the 1950s were not uniformly well received by the critics, there is no question that Ruiz Iriarte had achieved prominence in the theatrical world. Most of his works were presented throughout Spain and Spanish America as well as being translated to other languages. Not only did his plays star outstanding actors and actresses like Gascó, Carbonell, and Vico, but they were staged by noted directors like José Luis Alonso and Cayetano Luca de Tena. It was also in this period that Ruiz Iriarte began directing some of his own productions, a practice which he has continued up to the present time. Marion P. Holt includes him along with Miguel Mihura and José López Rubio on his list of playwright-directors of importance.[9]

It was likewise during the 1950s when three of Ruiz Iriarte's comedies were made into movies that he began a secondary career as a scriptwriter. *The Apprentice Lover* was filmed in Mexico while *Child's Play* and the historical farce *La guerra empieza en Cuba* [The war begins in Cuba] were produced by Spanish companies. Ruiz Iriarte does not consider his own work in the motion picture industry to be of great significance, but his activity as a writer of dialogue or collaborator on scripts has been a continual one for more than twenty years. Among his credits are *Una gran señora* [A great lady, 1959], based on a play by Enrique Suárez de Deza; *Mi noche de bodas* [My wedding night, 1961], from a story by André Solft and Istuan Bekeffi;

El secreto de Tomy [Tomy's secret, 1963], based on a novel by José
Mallorquí; and *Papá, mi caballo y tú* [Papa, my horse and you, 1963],
also from a novel by Mallorquí. Although the movies do not represent
important original work on the part of Ruiz Iriarte, they undoubtedly
afforded technical preparation for the television plays he was to write
starting in the mid-1960s.

In spite of his high level of productivity on his original plays and his
activity in the film industry, Ruiz Iriarte continued to contribute to
newspapers and magazines. His contribution to *Informaciones* in
Madrid and *El Noticiero Universal* in Barcelona dates from the 1950s
on. With seemingly boundless energy, he also began a series of play
adaptations. Among the works he has adapted for the Spanish stage
beginning in the mid 1950s are Terence Rattigan's *El príncipe durmiente* [The sleeping prince], Shakespeare's *La fierecilla domada*
[The taming of the shrew], Pedro Antonio de Alarcón's *El capitán
Veneno* [Captain Poison], Roussin's *Nina*, Schneider's *Las tres gracias de la casa de enfrente* [The three graces from the house across the
street], Lajos Zilhay's *La puerta abierta* [The open door], and Gabriel
Arout's *Manzanas para Eva* [Apples for Eve]. An additional original
comedy, *Elena, te quiero* [Elena, I love you], was written in collaboration with Janos Vaszary and Manuel Parada de la Puente.

Although Ruiz Iriarte maintained his high level of activity in writing for motion pictures and newspapers in the 1960s, he produced
fewer original plays than in the previous decade. For the first time
since he succeeded in having his works staged, there was a three-year
gap (1961–1963) with no new plays. It was during this period, however, that he published *Un pequeño mundo*, an anthology of twenty-
eight essays. Written in a polished style with a touch of humor, these
newspaper articles deal with a number of topics, some of which are
related to the author's work as a playwright: debunking the Don Juan
myth, social changes in postwar Spain, memories of his childhood,
travels in Spain and abroad, reaction to the French production of Jean
Anouilh's *The Lark*. They are subjective essays, reflecting Ruiz
Iriarte's personal experiences and his vision of a changing world.

In 1964 the playwright once again presented an original work on
the Madrid stage. *El carrusell* [The carousel] is a serious drama which
criticizes some of the same human weaknesses and societal changes
that he had lightly satirized in his earlier comedies of manners. It
introduced a series of mature works that must be considered among
the playwright's most important achievements: the light farce *Un*

paraguas bajo la lluvia [An umbrella under the rain], the comedy *La muchacha del sombrerito rosa* [The girl in the little pink hat], which won the National Literature Prize for 1967, and its sequel *Primavera en la plaza de París* [Springtime in the Plaza de París], winner of the María Rolland Prize for 1969; and two other serious dramas *La señora recibe una carta* [The lady receives a letter] and *Historia de un adulterio* [Story of adultery]. Ruiz Iriarte directed two of these plays himself while the others were staged by the noted actor-director Enrique Diosdado. Amelia de la Torre, who played the feminine lead in *The Girl in the Little Pink Hat*, *Springtime in the Plaza de París* and *Story of Adultery*, received the María Rolland Prize for best actress of the year for her work in the latter two plays.

In 1965 Ruiz Iriarte embarked upon a new and important area of literary activity. For Spanish television he began writing a series of short, original plays entitled *La pequeña comedia* [Little theater]. The following year he was awarded the National Television Prize for the series. By 1977 his original television scripts numbered over one hundred. Although writing for television involves a different technique than writing for the stage, Ruiz Iriarte believes that the creative process is similar; in his prologue to a published selection of the scripts he has expressed a strong defense of the literary and dramatic merits of television plays.

Long an active member of the Sociedad General de Autores de España, the association of Spanish writers, in 1969 Ruiz Iriarte was elected president of that organization, a position which he held for four and a half years. Currently he serves as president of the Montepío de Autores Españoles, the writers' pension fund.

During the 1970s, Ruiz Iriarte has maintained his active role in writing for television and movies, but his production of original stage plays has diminished considerably. Following a six-year period with no new plays, in 1975 he wrote and directed the comedy *Buenas noches, Sabina* [Good evening, Sabina]. In the summer of 1977 he began work on another play, which he hoped to stage in 1978. He has also continued his journalistic work, contributing regularly to the Madrid newspaper *ABC* and preparing a syndicated column for the EFE agency. Well written and marked by a gentle humor and irony, these recent essays are similar in style and tone to his earlier articles. They comment on aspects of a changing world from the problem of shoplifters in London and the astronomical salaries of soccer players in Germany to the recent Spanish trend toward fad diets and pornography. As always, Ruiz Iriarte is a perceptive observer, viewing the foibles of society from a mildly satirical perspective but without making harsh judgments.

III   *Ruiz Iriarte and the Post Civil War Theater*

In the 1940s, when Ruiz Iriarte first succeeded in having his plays staged, Spain was just emerging from the ashes of the Civil War. Some of the most promising younger playwrights from the prewar period were gone. Federico García Lorca (1898-1936) had been assassinated; Alejandro Casona (1903-1965) was in exile. Dominating the group of older playwrights who remained in Spain was the Nobel Prize winner Jacinto Benavente (1866-1954) who continued to produce comedies regularly until his death. Benavente's plays, and those of other writers of these years, were staged only if they were acceptable to the new government. Benavente's works tended to be both apolitical and repetitive of a kind of high comedy that he had developed long before the war. José María Pemán (b. 1898), a conservative, did not totally avoid social and political themes, but his ideology was consistent with that of the regime. Enrique Jardiel Poncela (1901-1952), the most innovative of the playwrights whose careers antedate the war, specialized in a kind of absurdist comedy far removed from religious or political considerations.

The postwar period reflected the impact of the civil conflict not only in terms of official censorship and the disappearance of some of the prewar playwrights but also in the composition of the theater-going public. Ruiz Iriarte himself notes that before the war there was a theater for the "masses" and a theater aimed at a select minority. Following the war, no such distinction remained, and playwrights began to realize that their public had never been the "masses" but rather a self-selected group (*T* 2:46). That group in the 1940s and 1950s was largely upper middle class and traditional. The liberal intellectuals who had formed the "select minority" of the 1930's were dead, silenced or in exile. The sector of the middle class that had triumphed in the war was characterized by "a certain traditionalism, a conservative attitude little given to daring, innovation, impudence." [10] The author who wanted to have his plays produced had to limit himself both to what censorship allowed and what the public wanted. In the wake of the Spanish Civil War, World War II, and the resultant economic and political situation in Spain, the self-selected group of theater-goers wanted an opportunity to escape from the social problems of the moment.

Ruiz Iriarte in his essays and interviews consistently shows himself to be a man knowledgeable about and sensitive to the history of world drama, the unique nature of his chosen genre, and the specific development of theater in Spain. For him, all theater is social whether it confronts reality or evades it: "The author is a consequence of his environment, an echo of his period; his voice and accent are, like it or not, the voice and the accent of the world that produces him." [11] For this reason, most theatrical works are quickly dated and do not pass on to posterity: "In the history of theater, the authors remain but the works disappear" (*T* 2:47). In postwar Spain, before the easing of censorship in the mid-1960s, there was "a theater that could be done and a theater that could not be done. Some of us authors have written over the years the theater that could be done. That does not mean that if we could have created the other theater, the one that could not be done, that we would not have written what we did anyway." [12]

The theater readily acceptable in those years after the war was light comedy, plays which might reflect reality but avoided the painful issues of the day. It was a kind of comedy Ruiz Iriarte personally admired and which he handled well, whether in the form of poetic fantasy or the more realistic comedy of manners. Ruiz Iriarte was the first new playwright of importance to appear in the Spanish theater in the 1940s and his early comedies actually precede the initial postwar productions of the older author with whom he is most frequently identified, José López Rubio (b. 1903). Two other writers of comedies sometimes grouped with Ruiz Iriarte and López Rubio in critical discussions of the contemporary theater are Edgar Neville (1899-1968) and, to a lesser extent, Miguel Mihura (1905-1977) but a complete list of the authors of light comedy staged in Spain in the two decades following the Civil War would be very extensive indeed. As Rodríguez Richart has noted, farce and light comedy are not new to the Spanish theater and, in fact, represent a very long literary tradition. [13]

The immediate Spanish precursors for the postwar writers of comedy were Benavente and Casona. Speaking of a group of playwrights, in which he includes López Rubio, Ruiz Iriarte, and Neville, Ignacio Soldevilla Durante observes: "They occupy a comfortable place on the stage, heirs to the brilliant, conversational theater, filled with happy expressions and subtle, not too malicious ironies, that came to them from Benavente and, at the same time, conscious of the lesson in dramatic technique and poetic fantasy of Casona." [14] The postwar writers could also turn for inspiration to foreign models in works of continental playwrights like Luigi Pirandello, Jean Giraudoux, Jean Anouilh, and such British writers as Noel Coward and Oscar Wilde. Enrique Sordo, for example, has found in López Rubio a joint influence of French and British literature and feels that, as a result, he has written an intellectual, civilized, correct theater. [15]

The theater created by these writers of comedies did not directly represent the political, social or economic reality of Spain but rather "was based on a desire to separate oneself from that reality." [16] "In this escapism, rooted in an anguished situation, in this brutal dissociation between reality and theater, between the man in the street and this same man turned into spectator, we would have one of the fundamental characteristics of the contemporary Spanish theater, established precisely when it seemed most difficult." [17]

The term "escapist" or "evasionist" theater very quickly became a catchword in Spain, frequently used in a negative sense. By 1949, with the première of Antonio Buero Vallejo's *Historia de una escalera* [Story of a stairway], Spain had found a new dramatic writer who was interested in dealing with contemporary reality and more concrete social questions. In the 1950s, with the emergence of Alfonso Sastre and the group of playwrights who formed the so-called "theater of protest," critics began to divide Spanish plays into categories of escapist and socially committed, the former often being rejected as frivolous and of no real literary or theatrical value. This negative attitude was reinforced, as José Monleón points out, by the inability of a younger generation that had not fully experienced the war to appreciate the war fatigue of the middle-class playgoer who initially hungered for escapist comedies. [18] Critical reactions to plays all too often became political judgments rather than literary ones, with works being labeled "escapist" or "rightist," "realistic" or "liberal" without regard for their individual merits within the context of theater itself.

Phyllis Hartnoll, in her history of world theater, observes both that "it is not necessary for the theater as a medium of entertainment to concern itself seriously with social problems" and that when audiences are willing to accept plays of social protest and criticism, "this may result in poor playwriting and in the production of a number of plays which, being nothing but propaganda, disappear without trace once their usefulness is over." [19] In other words, it is no more reasonable to assert that all "escapist" plays are worthless than it is to claim that all plays of "social protest" are worthy of study. Plays should be judged on their individual merits within the context of the particular subgenre to which they belong. Increasingly, critics of

Spanish theater have begun to apply this kind of literary evaluation to contemporary plays and also to reject the facile labels. It is from this perspective that Rodríguez Richart states: "It is known, in fact, that many of these theatrical works without great ambitions have turned out to be of higher quality, of greater perfection, than other 'committed' ones with grave problems in the background, with lofty goals, but lacking in interest, in tension, in fluidity, in a word, in the theatricality that a play must have in order to be good." [20] It is in a similar vein that Pérez Minik, in his discussion of López Rubio, Neville and Ruiz Iriarte, reminds his readers that at one time Marivaux's theater was considered artificial but that in recent times critics have discovered new merits in those same comedies. [21]

The belief that plays need not be realistic works of social protest in order to be of value does not represent a new discovery for Ruiz Iriarte himself. In the more than thirty years that he has expressed personal opinions on theater he has consistently defended comedy in general and the use of poetic fantasy in particular. In 1944 he wrote that the most beautiful theater he could imagine would be one in which an actor would direct himself to the audience at the beginning of the play and request that those incapable of dreaming leave. [22] Three years later in stronger tones he proclaimed: "The idea that in the theater nothing should happen that does not happen in life is a picturesque stupidity which, if it were true, would be the ruin of the undertaking." [23] During an interview in the mid-1960s he took a somewhat mellower position, indicating that all styles of theater have their own risks and that all of them are difficult to write. Agreeing with García Lorca, he affirmed that good and noble theater may be found in all of the subgenres from vaudeville to tragedy. "In my case, I will say that, in fact, at times I have felt sincere, very sincere, amused and even eloquent while I was writing some of those plays that have been called amiable comedies of manners. And never, in such a state, have I felt the anguish of someone who was frustrated halfway on a road. Because, simply, it was a different road that I had taken." [24]

In the decade of the 1960s Ruiz Iriarte turned his attention to serious drama and produced two works which in particular must be included among his most important plays. Nevertheless, up to the present he continues to consider himself with some pride primarily a writer of comedies:

I have written a good number of comedies. I have moved, I think, in this dramatic genre with love and with ease. Why? For the same reason that others find their best intellectual or sentimental adjustment in drama and still others in farce or vaudeville. In short, because each author fulfills his inexorable and mysterious destiny. Comedy is a beautiful dramatic style. It is, within theater, like a synthesis of theater. Inside its limits—wide, generous limits, to be sure—everything fits: laughter, emotion, ideas and the profound drama that is glimpsed and yet hidden among smiles. To comedy may be applied, perhaps better than to any other genre, the most beautiful and perfect definition of theater that I know: Theater is a game of the spirit.[25]

If Ruiz Iriarte's plays have not all been of equal merit neither have all critics been equally receptive to his kind of theater; yet there can be no question that he is one of the major playwrights of the post Civil War period. He is one of only a handful actively involved in the life of the Spanish stage for thirty or more years. Even those who reject his comedies as frivolous or insignificant acknowledge that he writes sparkling dialogue, is a skillful craftsman, and imbues his works with poetry, humor and tenderness. Some of his plays have been awarded major prizes and many of them have been commercial successes. Annually, Federico Carlos Sainz de Robles publishes an anthology of the Spanish plays staged in Madrid he judges to be the most important. In the twenty years from 1949-50 to 1968-69, he selected eleven of Ruiz Iriarte's works. For the same period Buero Vallejo is also represented by eleven and only Joaquín Calvo-Sotelo, with thirteen plays, appears more frequently.[26] Outside Spain, Ruiz Iriarte's theater has also attracted favorable attention in Central and South America, Europe and the United States.[27] Three of his full-length plays and a selection of his television plays are available in American student editions. Ranging from vaudeville and farce to serious drama, his complete works reveal a versatile playwright who has viewed society sometimes critically, sometimes sentimentally, but always with genuine concern and love for humanity. As the editors of the anthology *El teatro de 1950* have noted:

Víctor Ruiz Iriarte is one of the contemporary writers of comedies who best handles the threads of farce. Few know how as he does to place the tightrope of paradox over an abyss of truths and falsehoods. . . . The theater of Ruiz Iriarte reflects the amiable side of life, with doors and windows open to the lyric, the gently comic, the mildly satirical, to witty dialogue and to the lesson, midway between optimistic and sceptical, between moral and sentimental, of what the human heart is like.[28]

CHAPTER 2

Life as Theater:
The World of Poetic Fantasy

R UIZ Iriarte has frequently been identified as a playwright who
concentrates on the illusion-reality theme, developing characters who take refuge from harsh truths by creating for themselves and
others a world of poetic fantasy. Certainly this is the situation in *El
puente de los suicidas* [Suicide bridge], his first play to be staged
professionally, and in *El landó de seis caballos* [The six-horse landau],
one of his most successful comedies. It is largely because of these two
works that Ruiz Iriarte has been categorized as a writer of poetic
fantasy, but the same dominant tendency may be found in two other
comedies: *Academia de amor* [Academy of love] and *El café de las
flores* [The flowers cafe]. In each of these plays, one or more characters, in part to escape from the realities of his or her own existence
and in part for altruistic reasons, attempts to bring happiness to
others through illusion, often by establishing some sort of imaginative
institution.

These plays of poetic fantasy reflect the influence on Ruiz Iriarte of
several important twentieth century playwrights. Critics were quick
to note the ties between *Suicide Bridge* and Casona's *Prohibido
suicidarse en primavera* [Suicide prohibited in the spring]; Ruiz
Iriarte in fact, is often identified as one of Casona's followers. Like
Alejandro Casona (1903-65), the younger playwright's approach to
the reality-illusion theme bears a relationship to that of Pirandello as
well as to Anouilh, who was also influenced by the Italian. Less
frequently mentioned but perhaps more significant, particularly with
respect to *Suicide Bridge*, is the impact of Nicolai Evreinov and his
concept of theatricalized life. Ruiz Iriarte himself recognizes the
importance of both Casona and Evreinov on his earliest plays and
identifies Pirandello and Anouilh as great playwrights who have
strongly influenced contemporary European theater.[1]

I   Suicide Bridge

Although *Suicide Bridge* was first staged a year after the première of the one-act play *A Day in Glory*, it was written earlier and thus is the first of Ruiz Iriarte's plays extant.[2] The play opened in San Sebastián in June, 1944, followed by a Madrid production starring Tina Gascó in February, 1945. The time and place of the play's action are indefinite, the setting for act one being a bridge on the outskirts of any large city in the world and the other two acts taking place in a country home near that same unspecified city.

The action in act one takes place at night. Several groups of characters come and go on the bridge: an old blind beggar and the grandson who accompanies him, casual passersby, a pair of young lovers, a police detective and his superior, Daniel and Mary. Rapidly we learn that the bridge is a favorite spot for suicides, but that the police believe at least three of the "suicides" to be false: the cadavers for a bank teller accused of stealing a million *pesetas*, a young woman piano teacher who has had an unhappy love affair, and an elderly military officer living in exile have not been recovered. The police are determined to solve the mystery of the missing corpses.

Although the tone of some of the dialogue is comic, particularly that of the detectives and the innocent remarks of the child, we soon learn that the anguish of other characters is serious. The blind beggar attempts to commit suicide but is saved by the young lover. Mary, an adolescent, also tries to drown herself but is prevented from doing so by Daniel, a self-proclaimed "professor of happiness." He tells her that he will give her a new and splendid life and takes her away with him.

In act two we learn that Daniel, with the help of his servant Pedrín, has created a house of illusion for the three people he had earlier saved from suicide. Through phone calls and letters, Brummell, the bank teller, has been made to believe that he is the most powerful financier in the world. The General, who had been forced to retire because of ill health thus preventing him from receiving the promotion he had always dreamed of, now believes that popular support for him in his native land is so great that his king will soon proclaim him marshal. Like the two men, Isabel is blissfully happy, but the cause of her new contentment is not so readily observed. Only gradually does she reveal the secret that she has been receiving a daily love letter from an "unknown admirer"; she is sure both that the author is Daniel and that the love is real.

Mary's arrival initially threatens to destroy the happiness Daniel has created on the basis of illusion. Isabel, in her love for the professor of happiness, senses that the young girl is a rival. Mary, on the other hand, unwilling to accept illusion at all, declares that Daniel's treatment of his three protegés is a terrible farce. As act three opens, Mary tears the blindfold from Isabel's eyes, making her see the truth, and then flees in dismay at what she has done. Isabel in turn forces Brummell to see reality and attacks Daniel, telling him that he has ruined her life. Daniel protests that without him she would not even be alive. He prevents Brummell from leaving by pointing out to him that in the "real world" he is a wanted criminal. The confrontation is interrupted by the arrival of the police, who had seen Daniel rescue Mary the night before on the bridge. Rather than go to jail, Brummell kills himself with a gun he had taken from Pedrín's room.

Faced with the horror of Brummell's death, Isabel reverses her previous position; truth and reason have triumphed, but in doing so they have destroyed a man. When the General enters the room, she and the police join Daniel in humoring him so that the sick old man may remain happy in his dream world. Although Isabel decides to abandon Daniel's refuge, as Mary had done earlier, she subsequently returns, bringing with her the blind man whom she has just saved from a second suicide attempt. As the play ends, Isabel and Daniel determine that they will find happiness together while creating a world of poetic fantasy for the General and the beggar.

Although parallels between *Suicide Bridge* and the theater of Casona undoubtedly do exist, the specific similarity between Ruiz Iriarte's play and *Prohibido suicidarse en primavera* (1937) is, as Schevill has noted, "perhaps more superficial than real." [3] In Casona's play Doctor Roda is the director of Suicide House, a sanatorium for souls founded by Doctor Ariel. The House features a number of locations, ideally designed for killing oneself by drowning, poisoning, etc. But those who come there seeking death inevitably find that they prefer to live. Rather than save the potential suicides through illusion, as Daniel strives to do, Doctor Roda hopes to have them accept reality and adjust to it. In some cases the adjustment comes through a new love or friendship, but in no case is the patient saved through fantasy. *Suicide Bridge* is not merely a "new version" or inferior "imitation" of *Prohibido suicidarse en primavera*.[4] In its extended treatment of the illusion-reality theme, it bears a stronger relationship to Casona's earlier *La sirena varada* [The stranded mermaid, 1934], a similarity already pointed out by Valbuena Prat.[5] Probably because of their common ties to Evreinov, *Suicide Bridge* actually foreshadows Casona's later *Los árboles mueren de pie* [Trees die standing, 1949].[6]

Like Pirandello, with whose work in many respects his coincides, Nicolai Evreinov (1879-1953) rejected the realistic and naturalistic plays which dominated the stage at the end of the nineteenth century to develop instead a theater devoid of and opposed to such "illusionism" by introducing an element of poetry and fantasy. Both playwrights were interested in the relationship between illusion and reality in general and between theater and life in particular; Evreinov, however, placed greater stress on the concept of life as theater. Pirandello's characters are "estranged from life and enslaved by the mask and the role," while Evreinov's sought to escape reality: "we ought to be consciously, deliberately elaborating our illusions, creating theater in life, rather than leaving man naked in the name of murderous truth."[7] The play in which Evreinov most extensively elaborated on his concept of theatricalized life was *The Main Thing* (1921), a work staged by Pirandello in Italy in 1925 and translated to Spanish by Azorín in 1928 under the title *El doctor Frégoli o La comedia de la felicidad.*

The Main Thing is a highly complex play with a main character, Paraclete, who assumes various roles, including that of Dr. Fregoli. Having learned of the unhappy lives of two young people living in a boardinghouse, Dr. Fregoli hires three actors to assume roles in the theater of life and bring happiness to others. The Romantic Lead will be a boarder and pretend to love the landlady's daughter. His wife, the Barefoot Dancer, will play the role of a maid and pretend to love the student who has tried to commit suicide. The Comic will become another boarder, playing the role of a doctor and pretending to court another tenant, Aglaya Karpovna. Paraclete-Fregoli, now in the role of Schmidt, will also be among the boarders. The complicated plot includes illusions within illusions within illusions and ultimately comes to no conclusion. Paraclete, now in the guise of Harlequin, declares himself at a loss as to how to end the play and offers alternative solutions to the audience. Most relevant in terms of the impact on Casona and Ruiz Iriarte are the theory of Fregoli, perhaps shared by Evreinov, that "theatricalized life may improve upon reality" and the suggestion that "while the deception lasts, the people in difficulty actually find their lives improved."[8]

In *La sirena varada* Casona introduces a character, Ricardo, who at least initially appears to have a common bond with Dr. Fregoli and

Ruiz Iriarte's Daniel. Like Daniel, Ricardo has money and is able to afford his fantasies. With his faithful servant Pedrote, he moves to an isolated old house he hopes to turn into "an asylum for orphans from common sense." He declares at the beginning of the play that life is stupid and boring because we lack imagination and that he will identify a half dozen interesting people who have fantasy, but not sense, and will bring them together so that they may invent a new life.[9] The play as it develops, however, is more closely related to Pirandello than to Evreinov. Throughout much of the action Casona maintains a certain ambiguity, and neither the audience nor the other characters know who Sirena, the "mermaid," really is. We also do not know until the end of the play that Daniel, a painter who says he is wearing a blindfold so that he may better imagine colors, is, in fact, blind. Characters in the play do create illusions for themselves or for others—either humoring Sirena in her madness or humoring Ricardo in his whims—but they do so on a more limited, individual scale than Evreinov's Dr. Fregoli would recommend. While in Pirandello truth is relative and we cannot therefore distinguish clearly between illusion and reality, in Casona's play not only can we distinguish at the end but we also learn that the characters actually reject illusion in order to face reality itself. "Casona's conclusion is that the worlds of reality and happiness are synonymous." [10] The only character for whom this does not hold true in *La sirena varada* is Daniel.

Casona's *La sirena varada* may well be the point of departure for Ruiz Iriarte's *Suicide Bridge*, particularly in the initial parallel between Ricardo and Daniel, but Ruiz Iriarte's conclusions are different. His Mary, like Casona's Sirena-María and the majority of the characters in *La sirena varada*, does decide to confront reality, but for others illusion is the only viable alternative. When reason and truth intervene, Brummell kills himself. Daniel and Isabel are determined to protect the General and the old beggar from a similar fate.

Casona's philosophical position is consistent throughout the trilogy of illusion-reality plays. Like *La sirena varada*, *Prohibido suicidarse en primavera* and *Los árboles mueren de pie* conclude that one must accept life as it is—and that this is the way to achieve happiness. Like Evreinov, Ruiz Iriarte seems to take the opposite stand. It is on this basic level that *Suicide Bridge* differs most radically from *Prohibido suicidarse en primavera*. Casona's play has some relationship to Evreinov in the creation of doctors Ariel and Roda, who dedicate their lives to bringing happiness to others, and in the use of the sanatorium itself (which is really a large-scale stage setting) to achieve that goal. But Dr. Roda does not bring happiness through illusion as Evreinov's Dr. Fregoli or Ruiz Iriarte's Daniel attempt to do; rather his purpose is to restore people's will to live by "turning their souls rightside out." [11] Dr. Roda is generally aided in his efforts by the characters themselves who establish new bonds of affection with some other patient at the Suicide House. Of Ruiz Iriarte's three despondent attempted suicides, only one, Isabel, can be cured by love.

The obvious and most significant point of contact between Casona's *Prohibido suicidarse en primavera* and Ruiz Iriarte's *Suicide Bridge* is the theme of suicide. Dr. Roda explains to Fernando and Chole, a pair of happy lovers who arrive at the House by mistake, that Dr. Ariel founded the institution because in his own family there had been a history of suicides. Similarly Daniel explains to Isabel that he had seen his father kill himself and that he therefore wished to prevent others from taking their own lives. In Casona's play, when reality suddenly intervenes—Chole discovers that Fernando's brother Juan secretly loves her and suffers because of this—the result is an attempted suicide. In Ruiz Iriarte's play, when reality intervenes—the police arrive—Brummell does kill himself. But even here the two playwrights disagree philosophically. Casona has Chole recover, Juan refuses the charity of Chole's pretended love and finds happiness with another woman, and Chole and Fernando go back to their previous happy state. In Ruiz Iriarte's play, for Brummell there is no happy ending.

The play of Casona that most clearly shows the influence of Evreinov is *Los árboles mueren de pie*. This time Dr. Ariel has founded an organization which exists for the sole purpose of bringing happiness to others. Directed by Mauricio, the organization is like a theatrical troupe that creates illusions for any unhappy people it may find. Mauricio himself and Isabel, a young woman he has saved from suicide, agree to go to the home of Balboa to create an illusion for the old man's wife. The Grandmother must not learn that their absent grandson is a ne'er-do-well and that his letters over the years were really written by Balboa. Nor must she learn that the grandson is now supposedly dead and that Mauricio and Isabel are merely actors pretending to be the grandson and his wife. Both of these aspects of the plot, though directly related to situations in Evreinov's *The Main Thing*, are also quite similar to elements in Ruiz Iriarte's *Suicide Bridge*. Daniel, in his deliberate attempt to create a theatricalized life for the unfortunates he has rescued from suicide, is a "doctor of happiness" as is Mauricio. Daniel succeeds in persuading Isabel to join him in this charitable venture, and the pretended love he has shown her comes to be real. Similarly, when Mauricio takes Isabel with him on their venture into life as theater, their love, too, crosses the line between illusion and reality. In that Casona was living in exile in Argentina when Ruiz Iriarte wrote and staged *Suicide Bridge*, it is more likely that the parallels between the two works may be attributed to the common influence of Evreinov rather than to a direct influence of the younger playwright on Casona.

II Academy of Love

The third of Ruiz Iriarte's full-length plays to be staged, *Academia de amor* [Academy of love] which opened in San Sebastián in July, 1946, reached the Madrid stage in October of the same year. It subsequently was awarded the Piquer prize of the Spanish Royal Academy. Set quite concretely in Madrid, although at an indeterminate time, the action of the play takes place in an "academy of love" located at 162 Gran Vía. As act one opens, Luciano, accidentally stumbling upon the Academy, (which is for women only), learns that its director Madame Fleriot gives classes on love and helps women find happiness. Her motto for single women is that all of them can marry; for married women she proclaims that the "other woman" always loses. Fascinated by this mysterious "doctor of love," Luciano proceeds to research her past. In act two, he confronts her with his findings. Her real name is Paulina Rosas; for eighteen years she has led the life of an adventuress in the artists' colony of Paris, going by the name of Marguerite. Because he himself is basically a lonely, timid man, Luciano's purpose is not to blackmail Paulina; rather he seeks her affection. What he does not yet know but what the audience has come to suspect is that Paulina has come to Madrid to be near her daughter. She had abandoned her husband and her baby years before, and the girl has grown up believing her mother to be dead. Now Guillermina, who is among Paulina's young students, is being followed in the streets by the husband of one of Paulina's clients, Adela. To protect her daughter from seduction or disillusionment, Paulina is determined to restore happiness to the marriage of Adela and Fernando. By the end of the play she has done so, along with solving several other of the women's marital problems. At the conclusion she confides her whole story to Luciano and rejects any possibility of finding happiness with him in order to continue to watch over Guillermina and bring happiness to others.

In several respects *Academy of Love*, like *Suicide Bridge*, reflects the influence of Evreinov. As was true of Paraclete in *The Main Thing*, Paulina has several different identities; she also resembles him (in his guise of the Lady Fortune Teller) in her extraordinary talent for knowing just what people are really like and what their true problems really are—which in part is a consequence of her direct involvement in their lives. Luciano calls her a "doctor of love," but she might as easily be called a "doctor of happiness" as Ricardo in *Suicide Bridge* or Evreinov's Dr. Fregoli are known. To achieve happiness, she must believe strongly in the power of illusion. At the Academy itself, a stage setting of sorts, Paulina has cast herself in the role of Madame Fleriot. Her advice to her clients very often hinges on their assuming certain roles. Adela, to help in reclaiming Fernando's love, must be "a bit of an actress" and, if she cannot learn how to lie, she will lack the prerequisite for happiness.[12] Another client, Cecilia, has successfully won back an unfaithful husband by playing sick. Tomás, the husband of Diana, who has pretended to take a lover in order to get even with her husband for his infidelity, is advised to pretend to believe her story in order to restore happiness to their marriage. Paulina tells Luciano that her own husband has found peace and has forgiven her because "he loves me as if I really were dead" (*A*, 152). Certainly Guillermina has accepted her father's illusion as being real. The young woman is convinced that the widower's continued devotion to his bride is an example of ideal love (*A*, 119, 121). Paulina's philosophy is that one may achieve happiness through the use of theater in life. As she tells her companion Cristina, people are fascinated by myths and myths are very easy to invent. For the women who enter the Academy door, she can create new destinies (*A*, 107).

While *Academy of Love* reveals Ruiz Iriarte's continued interest in Evreinov's concept of theatricalized life, it also bears some relationship to the works of Luigi Pirandello (1867-1936). Though the possible influence of Pirandello on twentieth-century Spanish playwrights has been the subject of considerable critical debate, relatively little has been written about the Pirandellism of Ruiz Iriarte.[13] In a superficial way Pirandello, with his emphasis on the illusion-reality theme, is linked to a long Hispanic tradition, including such writers as Cervantes and Calderón. But Pirandello is distinguished by his use of ambiguity and irony and by his prevalent pessimism. The line between illusion and reality, between art and life, is difficult to define because truth itself is relative. Each individual may have his or her own concept of truth, but even the "true" identity of that individual may be impossible to grasp because we each wear a series of masks. Ruiz Iriarte, like Casona, does not share Pirandello's underlying pessimism, but certain of his plays lie well within the Pirandellian mode.[14] The tendency was already apparent in *Suicide Bridge*. When Isabel accuses Daniel of having destroyed her life, Daniel in Pirandellian fashion responds by asking whether she even exists, "What is your life? Are you alive?" [15] Because he has saved her from self-destruction, he considers her existence to be his work. Reality may indeed be unbearable, as Isabel, who voluntarily returns to Daniel's house of illusion, learns.

In *Academy of Love*, the Pirandellian theme is even more developed than in *Suicide Bridge*. Paulina's success with her Academy is dependent not upon what she really is but by what people assume her to be. Appearance is more important than "reality," but what is the reality of Paulina? What is the woman's true identity? A young bride and mother? The woman who abandoned her family? The woman of easy virtue who dominated the Parisian artists' colony? The wise fairy godmother who resolves marital conflicts and watches over her own daughter? The authentic Paulina, the one who rejects Luciano's offer of love and appears to find peace in her role as Madame Fleriot, is much closer to the role she has created in Madrid in the present than to the role of Marguerite she played in her eighteen years as an adventuress in France. Paulina does not, however, attempt to inject her vision of herself into the illusion that her husband has created. Guillermina and her father are happier with the "truth" as they see it than they could possibly be with Paulina's "truth." Ruiz Iriarte's character seems to adopt the Pirandellian concept expressed in his play *It Is So (If You Think So)*. She is not tempted to reveal her true identity to her daughter as is a similar mother in Pirandello's *As Well As Before, Better Than Before* who finds herself in the role of stepmother after her return. Also somewhat Pirandellian is the complex relationship of Diana and Tomás. As a response to the husband's infidelity, the wife imagines a love affair of her own and then contemplates suicide. In order to restore happiness to their marriage, the husband must pretend to believe the wife's story of infidelity so that she, in turn, can take pity on his anguish and reveal to him the truth. Although Paulina upon his arrival tells Tomás that she has seen through Diana's lie, the audience probably has not. Thus a kind of Pirandellian ambiguity with respect to the Diana-Tomás relationship is maintained throughout much of the action of the play.

Although *Academy of Love* belongs to a rather small group of Ruiz Iriarte's plays in which poetic fantasy dominates, it introduces several themes and character types which recur with frequency throughout his theater. The battle of the sexes and particularly domestic relations form the basis of a number of his comedies. Emphasis on love and its importance to human happiness, a theme already expressed by Isabel in *Suicide Bridge*, likewise is present in many of his works.[16] Both Luciano and Paulina anticipate certain characters who repeat themselves in some of his comedies of the 1950s. Luciano, in his timidity, his loneliness, and his nonconformity—he works only part of the day as an insurance salesman and spends the rest of his time simply wandering around Madrid, contemplating life—has much in common with the masculine figures identified by Arcadio Baquero Goyanes as the *"pobre hombre"* or *"pobrecito,"* a poor fellow or wretch who does not match up to society's expectations for a man.[17] Like his counterparts in the later comedies, Luciano is a charming character who undoubtedly wins the sympathy of the audience. Paulina is the first in a series of characters who allow Ruiz Iriarte to introduce "inverted value judgments of people, accepted customs, and social prejudices."[18] Paulina, a woman who has abandoned her own husband and baby and has undoubtedly had many lovers, would seem like the last person to give advice on love to virtuous young Spanish girls and wives. But yet she has great wisdom, sensitivity, and goodness of heart. She wishes other women, particularly her own daughter, to be happy and is willing to sacrifice herself to achieve that end. In the case of Paulina, as with many of his subsequent characters, including the *pobrecito*, Ruiz Iriarte will ask us to set aside our initial prejudices and seek the authentic person under the surface appearance.

III   The Six-Horse Landau

The best known of Ruiz Iriarte's plays of poetic fantasy, *El landó de seis caballos* [The six-horse landau] opened in Madrid in May, 1950, and was the work with which "the playwright's reputation was firmly established."[19] Because the basic theme concerns the relationship between illusion and happiness, *The Six-Horse Landau* has been called a prototype of "evasionist theater."[20] Although the latter label often carries a pejorative sense, in this case it was never a hindrance to the generally favorable reaction the play has earned. Alfredo Marqueríe, like many critics, found the comedy to excel in its use of fantasy, poetry, tenderness and humor.[21] Isabel Schevill has termed it "a masterpiece of intranscendental playfulness." [22]

The action takes place within the space of a few hours in an isolated old country home in the province of Avila. As the play opens three old people, dressed in the style of the early 1900s—Doña Adelita, Chapete, and Simón—are taking a ride in an imaginary landau which they have fashioned from sofas. A fourth old person, Pedro, who is carrying a balloon, enters and scolds them for their lack of seriousness. Into this whimsical scene walks Margarita, a very modern and stylish young woman. She has come to the estate at the written invitation of the Duke, but neither she nor the audience understands who or what the zany old people are and where the Duke might be. Margarita's arrival is followed by that of several other young people who have been invited by the Duke: Rosita, a flower girl; Isabel, an elegant young woman; Florencio, a scholarly archeologist; and Bobby, a musician who has been hired for the occasion. The three women have all come with illusions about the Duke's intentions and thus immediately perceive each other as rivals. Florencio has come in hopes of having the Duke establish an archeological institute. Not until the end of the play do they learn from Doña Adelita that the Duke has been dead for five years or why they have been invited.

Years before, Chapete, the Duke's coachman, had had an accident with a horse and had hit his head. For him time has stood still. He believes that it is 1903 and that he and Adelita will soon be married. The other three, with the aid of the Duke, have humored him in his madness for so long and so well that now only Doña Adelita is able to distinguish between reality and fantasy. The four have found happiness, playing as children do. At will they can take carriage rides, see the Queen pass by, visit Aranjuez, have a picnic—all without leaving the house. At the Duke's death, he left Adelita with the letters she might eventually send to find someone to take her place; knowing that she will soon die, she asked the doctor, who never appears on stage, to select some prospects for her.

The five puzzled guests who had wondered what the link among them was, now find out. The doctor is the father of Margarita's illegitimate child and the man who has attempted to seduce Rosita. He is also Isabel's cousin, Florencio's old classmate, and the man who hired the musician. Once the truth is known, Margarita, Rosita and Bobby leave—the latter two together, and Margarita in pursuit of the doctor. But Isabel, who has never had anyone love her and who has written letters to an imaginary sweetheart, is enchanted by the poetry of the old people's life and has decided to stay and assume Doña Adelita's role. Florencio, who finds for the first time that he can talk to a woman, believes that they are kindred souls and apparently will join Isabel in bringing happiness to the old men. Certainly there is a strong escapist theme in the work, with most of the characters, both young and old, willing to believe in illusions at least temporarily as a means of overcoming their own reality. Although Margarita and Rosita do accept reality when they find that the Duke does not exist, for the fanciful Isabel illusion is stronger than even the possibility of romance. She is happy to have found Florencio, but not willing to abandon the poetic world of the old people.

With the old people themselves, the escapist theme is developed on two levels: the replacement of reality by imagination and even madness, and the replacement of the present by the past. In both respects, *The Six-Horse Landau* is related to a number of Spanish plays of the late 1940s and early 1950s that deal with illusion. In Soriano de Andia's *Ayer . . . será mañana* [Yesterday . . . will be tomorrow, 1951], for example, one of the characters keeps alive the year 1909, complete with an elaborate stage setting, in juxtaposition with the present. In *María Antonieta* [Marie Antoinette, 1952], Joaquín Calvo-Sotelo has created a serious drama that deals with the dual themes of time and madness. But the play which probably bears the greatest similarity to *The Six-Horse Landau* is José López Rubio's *La venda en los ojos* [The blindfold, 1954]. Beatriz has been deserted by her husband. Rather than admit that he is not coming back, she retreats into feigned madness and stops time. Each day she goes to the airport to meet him. Her elderly aunt and uncle humor her in her madness, creating a whimsical world of illusion not unrelated to that in *The Six-Horse Landau*, and involve outsiders as well in their theatricalized life. When Beatriz finds a new love, however, she willingly reenters reality.[23]

The dual themes of time and madness are also the link connecting Ruiz Iriarte's comedy and Pirandello's *Enrico IV*, [Henry IV, 1922]. In the Italian play, the protagonist had hit his head when his horse fell. At the time of the accident, he was participating in a masquerade and was dressed in the role of the German king. In his resultant madness, having believed himself to be the medieval figure, over the years he has been humored by servants and friends who obligingly assume historical roles. Typical of Pirandello's theater, however, it is difficult to distinguish between reality and illusion, sanity and madness. Although the other characters assume that Henry IV is mad, in fact his insanity was only temporary. He has continued to pretend madness in order to amuse himself at the expense of those who participate in the elaborate farces staged in his behalf. But at the conclusion of the play, when he kills the man who in real life stole the woman he loved, Henry IV is forced into adopting forever the mask he formerly wore voluntarily.

Holt is quite correct in asserting that Chapete's accident with his resultant madness in *The Six-Horse Landau* openly reveals its antecedent in Pirandello's play.[24] One might also note that Ruiz Iriarte's Duke had shut himself up in his estate in 1910 because of a duel, an aspect of the story also clearly related to the end of *Henry IV*. Although the Spanish playwright, beyond these obvious borrowings in the plot, develops a juxtaposition of past and present, madness and sanity, illusion and reality, *The Six-Horse Landau* is not really Pirandellian in tone or intent. "Ruiz Iriarte's characters are obviously living a more sentimental or poeticized play-within-a play" than are Pirandello's.[25] Gone is the pessimism of *Henry IV*. For Doña Adelita and Isabel it is quite possible to find happiness by creating illusions for others. The old people are like children who find pleasure in their games, and when they tire of one game, they can always play at something else.[26] Florencio and Isabel, too, have this childlike capacity for make-believe, hence are able to fall in love while sitting under an almond tree the old people have brought in to be the "country" on a rainy day. *The Six-Horse Landau*, with its stress on the possibility of achieving happiness through illusion, is closer in tone to Evreinov than to Pirandello; but here Ruiz Iriarte is developing more the concept of life as a game than life as theater. When the characters assume roles for themselves or for others, they do so not self-consciously as actors but rather like children, embarked spontaneously on a game of "let's pretend."

Among the playwrights Ruiz Iriarte himself most admires is Jean Anouilh (1910—). Also heavily influenced by Pirandello, Anouilh nevertheless has written some plays, notably his *pièces roses* (pink plays) and *pièces brillantes* (brilliant plays), where the endings are happy and the tragic implications of the situations he describes are played down. Such is the case of his *Léocadia* (1939), a play with which *The Six-Horse Landau* has much in common both in plot and tone. The Prince has loved the actress Léocadia, who had died a sudden and unfortunate death. In response to this loss, he has retreated from reality; for him, time has stood still. His aunt, the Duchess, has humored him in his madness and has had the places he visited with Léocadia reconstructed in her gardens so that he may constantly relive the past. Amanda, a seamstress who bears a strong physical resemblance to the dead actress, is brought by the Duchess to her country home to assume the role of Léocadia and bring happiness to the Prince. Ultimately we learn that the Prince is not really mad but has been pretending; he and Amanda fall in love and presumably find happiness. Ruiz Iriarte's play resembles Anouilh's in several obvious ways. The themes of time and madness are presented here as in *Henry IV*, but the possibility of happiness exists. The humble Amanda, when she reaches the Duchess' home, is very much like Rosita in her arrival at the Duke's estate. Both plays also are far more comic than Pirandello's; Ruiz Iriarte has, in fact, called his own a poetic farce. It is quite reasonable to assume that there are traces of both Pirandello and Anouilh in the Spanish play, with the light-hearted tone of the Spanish work more nearly resembling the latter than the former.[27]

All three of the women who come to the Duke's house, as well as Florencio, are characters whose lives could have been developed with tragic undertones. In one way or another, they are lonely or disillusioned.[28] The story of Doña Adelita and Chapete, too, could have been handled on a very different level. But because Ruiz Iriarte in *The Six-Horse Landau* chose to write a "poetic farce," the play is by far the most obviously comic of the four works discussed in this chapter. The playwright has exploited to the fullest comic potential: the contrast between the anachronistic old people and their unexpected guests, the confusion of the young people themselves when they are confronted by this incongruous and mad world of illusion, the perpetual squabbles of the old men, and the rivalry of the three women for the affection of the mythical Duke.

The Six-Horse Landau has a number of points of contact with *Suicide Bridge* and *Academy of Love*. Florencio, like Luciano of *Academy of Love* is a *pobrecito*, a shy man who has never had any success with women. Isabel, like Isabel of *Suicide Bridge*, is a romantic, a woman capable of writing letters to an imaginary lover or falling in love with the mythical writer of false letters. Nevertheless, in all three plays, illusion and the creation of happiness for others take precedence over the possibility of obtaining romantic love for oneself. The endings of *The Six-Horse Landau* and *Suicide Bridge* are virtually identical in the relationship developed between Florencio-Isabel and Ricardo-Isabel. In *Academy of Love*, Paulina rejects Luciano's love entirely. Even more significant than these similarities, however, is the basic formula Ruiz Iriarte develops in all three of the plays and which he will partially use again in *The Flowers Cafe*. In each case one or more characters within the play have created a fanciful kind of institution: a house of illusion for attempted suicides, an academy of love, a "kingdom of the imagination." [29] Into this strange and bewildering setting comes an outsider—María, Luciano, or all five guests of the Duke—whose initial astonishment leads both to some comic confusion and to an explanation for the benefit of that character and the audience. Essentially this is also the formula for Casona's trilogy: *La sirena varada, Prohibido suicidarse en primavera,* and *Los árboles mueren de pie.* But in the development of their formula, Ruiz Iriarte and Casona consistently reach different conclusions. While Casona's characters dissolve the institutions because they cause more harm than good, Ruiz Iriarte's elect to perpetuate them for the sake of the happiness illusion can bring.

IV The Flowers Cafe

El café de las flores [The flowers cafe] opened in Madrid in October, 1953, and starred Tina Gascó, the same actress who created Isabel in the Madrid production of *Suicide Bridge*. Chronologically the play falls within the period of the "comedies of manners" and bears certain similarities to them. [30] However, because the play deals with the creation of an illusion on a large scale in order to bring happiness to a group of people, it may appropriately be grouped with the other works of poetic fantasy. The first act takes place at 3:00 A.M. at a sidewalk cafe. [31] The cafe is now closed, but not totally abandoned. César, an unsuccessful painter, is there, trying to sleep with dignity. Marta, a young woman carrying a suitcase, comes and goes, obviously waiting for someone who should have arrived long before. Cris, a poor cigarette girl, enters, trying to sell her wares. But the focus of attention is Laura, an elegant and attractive woman who is suffering her first night of loneliness. She ultimately decides to remove the loneliness all of them suffer. By the time the first act has concluded, she adds to the collection of unfortunates she gathers Pepe, an old cab driver, and Chico, a young man who up to the present has survived by stealing. Like Ricardo in *Suicide Bridge*, Laura is wealthy and can afford to implement her altruistic plan. If life excludes those who lack companionship, then she will take these outcasts to her home where they can be happy together. She will establish "a world apart." [32] They will form "a new family" (C, 71).

This opening act of the play is marked by the same sparkling dialogue and skillful use of comic techniques Ruiz Iriarte tends to develop throughout his theater. Particularly effective here is the incongruous humor of César, an apparent vagabond, haughtily demanding that others respect his peace and privacy so that he may sleep. Also well handled is the gradual sense of solidarity among the lonely characters. By the time Marta returns to tearfully confess to the others that she is alone in the world, Cris can respond with a clap of the hands and a cry of "Bravo! Bravo!" (C, 25). In a clever comic reversal, Ruiz Iriarte has turned loneliness from a negative to a positive value. Unlike the first act of *The Six-Horse Landau*, however, the comic techniques here do not overshadow the anguished reality of the various characters.

Ruiz Iriarte displays in this first act and throughout *The Flowers Cafe* the same careful craftsmanship apparent in the other plays in this group. In the first act of *Suicide Bridge*, he presented the mystery of the missing suicides. The audience is not given the solution, but one can guess the connection between Ricardo and the mystery. In the second act, our suspicions are confirmed. In the third act, the inevitable resolution of the conflict necessarily occurs when the police learn what we already know to be true. A similar plot outline obtains for *Academy of Love*. In act one we do not know—but can suspect that—the mysterious Madame Fleriot is the mother of Guillermina. In the second act, our suspicions are confirmed, but our interest is maintained through the conclusion of the play as to the resolution of Guillermina's situation and Madame Fleriot's true identity. In this first act of *The Flowers Cafe* we learn that Marta had planned to run away with a man who failed to meet her at the agreed upon time and place. Laura does not tell us that the man is her husband Gonzalo, who has abandoned her for a new love, but there are ample indications that such is the case. In act two, when Laura's new friends are all happily settled in her home, she reveals her own story to Marta, but without suggesting that Marta's boyfriend and Laura's husband are the same person. The audience, of course, is prepared both for the inevitable revelation of Gonzalo's identity and for a third act in which the conflict must be resolved.

In the other three plays of poetic fantasy, Ruiz Iriarte utilizes a formula in which an outsider, to his astonishment, suddenly finds himself in the middle of a most fanciful institution. In *The Flowers Cafe* the playwright increases the comic effect by having the "outsider" be Laura's husband. When Gonzalo returns to his wife the day after his departure, he finds that his home is now a refuge for a group of strangers and that not only does he not belong but he must pretend not to be Laura's husband as well. Like Ricardo in *Suicide Bridge*, Laura has created illusions to fill the void in other characters' existences. No longer believing himself to be a failure, César has begun again to paint, filling the house with canvases of dubious merit. Cris, an illegitimate child whose mother died leaving her orphaned, now has a new mother in Laura. Marta had quit her job to run away with Gonzalo, but now at least she has a home and friends. Laura is not willing to destroy these illusions by having the others learn that she no longer shares their common loneliness: "They are asleep and I don't want them to wake up" (*C*, 62). When Gonzalo asks her what will happen when they do learn the truth, Laura replies, "I don't know. I don't want to know. I only know how much a few hours of happiness are worth in certain lives" (*C*, 62). Laura's concept, like that of Evreinov's Dr. Fregoli, is that illusion can bring at least a temporary respite from harsh reality.

The action of the third act is complicated by a double love triangle. Although she still does not know that Gonzalo is Laura's husband, Marta has come to realize that Gonzalo loves Laura. Gonzalo, on the other hand, has learned that César, whom he has disliked from the beginning, is in love with Laura. These conflicts have not yet been resolved when Laura's guests accidentally learn the true relationship between her and Gonzalo. Much to Laura's sincere dismay, they all leave. "Why are we not able to make others happy?" she asks. "Can't we dream? Can we not face sorrow with a little imagination? Must life be as it is: dirty, ugly and sad?" (*C*, 87). The answer to her question is not clearcut. Marta and Gonzalo are gone for good, but Cris, Pepe and Chico return, presumably to find continued happiness with Laura and Gonzalo. For Laura, Cris is the nicest dream of all, "the dream of a daughter that I don't have" (*C*, 88).

There are obvious ties between *The Flowers Cafe* and other plays by Ruiz Iriarte. The marital troubles of Laura and Gonzalo are similar to problems brought to Madame Fleriot in *Academy of Love* as well as to the basic plots of several of the comedies of manners. César, although less timid than Luciano and Florencio, is related to the *pobrecito* figure. Cris, with a gift for fantasy that has allowed her to create an imaginary father, is linked to the Isabels of *Suicide Bridge* and *The Six-Horse Landau*. Laura has much in common not only with the protagonists of the poetic fantasy plays who wish to bring happiness to others but also with a series of strong, admirable female characters found repeatedly in Ruiz Iriarte's theater.

As a group, the four plays of poetic fantasy rank high among Ruiz

Iriarte's achievements, certainly for the early years of his career as a playwright. While several of his plays produced before 1950 were relative failures and have never been published, the works of poetic fantasy, including the prize winning *Academy of Love* and the highly successful *The Six-Horse Landau*, earned Ruiz Iriarte a considerable reputation. They are works characterized by careful construction and excellent craftsmanship, particularly in the use of comic techniques. For Ángel Valbuena Prat these plays, which create a poetic world in which one may overcome reality, are superior to the comedies of manners which in the following decade predominate.[33] While "escapist" plays in the sense that they deal with the desire of the characters themselves to escape from the bounds of reality, they are also works which deal with illusion and happiness themes on a universal plane and may be related to the works of important playwrights outside Spain, such as Pirandello, Evreinov, and Anouilh, as well as to Casona and other Spanish writers.

CHAPTER 3

The Satirical Farces

R UIZ Iriarte generally tends to view life with neither laughter nor
tears, but rather with a smile.[1] Absent from his work is the bitter
or grotesque satire of a Quevedo or Valle-Inclán. Nevertheless in
many of his plays there is an underlying if somewhat subdued satirical
intent. Pérez Minik, who groups him with López Rubio and Edgar
Neville as one of three "doctors of reality," finds that Ruiz Iriarte is
the one who "remains most within the classic tradition of comedy as a
means of correcting social customs and vices." [2] Certainly in both his
comedies of manners of the 1950s and in his more serious commentar-
ies on contemporary life of the 1960s, there is an element of satire
aimed specifically at Spanish society. Three of his farces—*Un día en
la gloria* [A day in glory], *El gran minué* [The grand minuet], and *La
cena de los tres reyes* [The dinner of the three kings]—fall into neither
of those two categories and may be viewed separately as comedies of
satire.[3]

I A Day in Glory

A one-act farce, *Un día en la gloria* [A day in glory] was Ruiz
Iriarte's first play to be staged. Both the production in Zaragoza in
September, 1943, and that in Madrid of July, 1944, were the work of
university groups, not professional actors. The action is set in the
mythical realm of Glory and the characters are dominantly historical
or legendary figures of different places and times: Joan of Arc, Sarah
Bernhardt, Don Juan, Napoleon. There is an experimental and imaginative quality about the work which sets it quite apart from any of
Ruiz Iriarte's other published plays.[4] The playwright makes use of the
inhabitants of his Glory to create an atmosphere of farce. The characters and their costumes are intended to be exaggerated and to stand in
comic contrast to one another. The Herald, whose trumpet calls
people to Glory each daybreak, is to be outfitted with "imagination

and fantasy." [5] The Chamberlain, dressed like a cossack guard from the court of Nicolas II, should appear "extravagant" (D, 75).

Aside from juxtaposing such diverse figures as a fakir, a Spanish bandit, a saint, and a popular singer, Ruiz Iriarte achieves a comic effect by debunking the myths surrounding some of his historical or legendary characters. The bandit has found a billfold and hopes to return it to its owner. Don Juan pursues a singer who is totally uninterested in him and tells him that he is outdated, ugly and has poor taste (D, 82). Sarah Bernhardt insults Don Juan further by assuring him that "romantic girls dream about you because they've never seen you. The truth is that up close you lose quite a bit." (D, 83). Ruiz Iriarte's point, which ultimately is expressed by the Chamberlain, is that those who inhabit Glory are merely shadows reflecting what people on earth remember them to have been. In truth, they do not exist. Glory is a whim of the masses, and hence includes the great philosophers side by side with the songstresses and the football heroes (D, 91).

But the real object of Ruiz Iriarte's satire in A Day in Glory is not so much Glory itself but the contemporary world. The Herald finds his situation ridiculous. Each morning he blows his trumpet, but now no one answers. Daybreak is the hour for dreams, but modern man sleeps through until 8:00, gets up, and does his exercises (D, 78). Sports are therefore destroying dreams, claims the Chamberlain who worries that Glory will have to close (D, 78, 84). Napoleon and Don Juan agree that the twentieth century is a time which rejects ambition, heroism and imagination (D, 84).

When a new arrival finally does reach Glory, his presence only reinforces the pessimistic view of contemporary society. The hero of the moment is a Hollywood star, Robert Lorry. Because of his success in the movies, he has become a millionaire and an "authority" on foreign policy (D, 86). Young men all try to look like him and young women are all in love with him (D, 92). When Napoleon learns that Lorry's latest triumph, one which earned him entrance to Glory, was a portrayal of Napoleon himself, but so distorted from historical truth as to offend the Emperor deeply, Napoleon abandons Glory to seek instead refuge in Limbo. The contemporary "heroes" in an unheroic time are mere actors who acquire fame by "parodying the adventure of those who fought on earth for immortality" (D, 93). [6]

II   The Grand Minuet

While A Day in Glory is a modest, experimental one-act play, Ruiz

Iriarte's second satirical comedy, *El gran minué* [The grand minuet], which calls for a lavish stage production, proved to be one of his important commercial successes. Gerald E. Wade points out that it was a theatrical spectacle and suggests that "it was this fact, as much as the play's excellence as drama, that made of it perhaps the most talked about comedy that Iriarte has written." [7] Termed by its author a "farce-ballet," the play opened in Madrid in December, 1950.

The action of the play takes place in the early eighteenth century at an unidentified European court that is obviously Versailles. The play opens with a prologue presented by Diana, who tells us that we are about to witness a double theatrical game: the minuet itself and also the farce. The characters are like figurines on a music box or little dolls in an old engraving that suddenly come to life. [8] The prologue is one of the few occasions in Ruiz Iriarte's theater where he has deliberately broken the illusionism of the stage, alerting the audience from the beginning that what we are about to see is not "reality." The brief introduction has been compared by Holt to a similar prologue in Jacinto Benavente's satirical farce *Los intereses creados* [The bonds of interest, 1907] where Crispín tells us that what follows is a mere puppet play. [9] In their prologues the playwrights deliberately mislead us, for both Ruiz Iriarte's minuet and Benavente's puppets are metaphors for the game of life.

Central to the plot are Diana, the innocent and unsophisticated young woman who is the current mistress of the King; the idealistic Valentín, who has come from his village to save Diana and the Court from immorality; and Nicolás de Gravelot, the cynical prime minister who is actually the power behind the throne. In the course of the play Diana becomes aware of the power she holds and, following her first ball, is seduced by the magic of the Court. In turn she literally seduces Valentín, who loses his idealism along with his innocence. The result saddens Gravelot, who had seen in Valentín not so much a political enemy as a personification of the idealistic political figure he might himself have been. Valentín is now just another dancer in the "grand minuet of the Court." History has repeated itself, he laments. Another idealistic young poet has died and another cynical philosopher has been born (*G*, 190).

In keeping with the farcical tone of the play, Ruiz Iriarte introduces a number of secondary figures who are caricatures. Diana, surrounded by a chorus of lively if immoral ladies-in-waiting, is being prepared for life at Court by a comic tutor and music instructor. At the ball she meets a trio of the King's former mistresses, one of whom ran a liberal government, one a conservative government, and one who simply did not remain in power long enough to affect history. The King is advised by a comic group of inept ministers, including a minister of war who is a pacifist because wars destroy gardens. But it is the King himself who stands as the major caricature of the farce. Called Carlitos by his mistress and ridiculed by his pages, the King lets Gravelot govern because he himself is incapable of doing so. Typically in character is the way in which he met Diana, the country girl: "I found the King there one morning, lost in the woods. The poor little fellow had become separated from his hunting party and all he could do was sneeze . . . If I hadn't come along, he would have been left like a little bird" (G, 128). The absolute monarch is Ruiz Iriarte's *pobrecito* figure carried to the extreme. History will never know this, however. Gravelot will take care of that. As he tells Diana, "My dear! We all know that His Majesty is not very intelligent. But don't worry. This secret will never leave the Court. His Majesty will pass into History as a great King, absolute, powerful and talented" (G, 119).

Ruiz Iriarte's intent quite clearly is to debunk the myth of the all-powerful king who rules by divine right. In his playful approach to history and in his humor, he shows a relationship to certain plays of Jean Giraudoux or Jean Anouilh. In Giraudoux's *La Guerre de Troie n'aura pas lieu* [The Trojan War will not take place, 1935], for example, there is also a systematic demythification process, and the great minds of Troy, like the King's advisers in *The Grand Minuet*, are comic figures. A reference to the same Greek legend appears in Ruiz Iriarte's play when one of Diana's companions conjectures that Valentín may turn out to be a foreign prince who has fallen in love with the King's mistress. Eagerly she predicts: "One night he will steal you away and there will be a war. You will be Helen of Troy. What luck!" (G, 113). Ruiz Iriarte's minister of war gives the same reason for his pacifism as does Giraudoux's gardener in his *Electre* (1937).[10] The concern that Gravelot and Diana express for the position they and the King will hold in history is like the self-conscious preoccupation one finds in the historical and legendary characters of both Giraudoux and Anouilh. Ruiz Iriarte is also linked to the latter playwright in his use of the minuet as a backdrop to the action of his play. Anouilh, particularly in his lighter plays, has frequently used both the concept of theater as a game and ballet or dance as a structural device. The very titles of some of his comedies indicate this tendency: *Le Bal des voleurs* [The thieves' ball, 1932], *La Valse des toréadors* [The toreadors' waltz, 1951]. *L'Invitation au chateau* [Invitation to the chateau, 1947] not only includes a kind of choreogra-

phy like the minuet scene of Ruiz Iriarte's farce but similarly deals
with the presentation in high society of a beautiful young woman of
the lower class.

Although *The Grand Minuet* debunks the myth of the absolute
monarch, the real object of Ruiz Iriarte's satire is not royalty but
political power. The playwright himself rejects the comment of some
critics that *The Grand Minuet* is an antimonarchist work. Had he
intended to attack royalty *per se*, he assures us that he would not have
done so through such a "foolish and tender" caricature of a king. [11]
Indeed though Carlitos is a comic figure he is not subject to the kind
of grotesque deformation one finds in certain works of Valle-Inclán. [12]
Ruiz Iriarte concentrates rather on power as a corrupting force and on
the weaknesses in human nature which prevent the triumph of good.
Diana's tutor tells her that "Power is a dream that does not allow one
to dream because it makes possible all dreams" (G, 111). Power thus
destroys illusions and idealism. Diana, who is initially depicted as
virtuous and quite unaware that the relationship between her and the
King is a sin, dreams of making the Court and her ladies-in-waiting
"decent." But once she understands her own situation and her own
power, she becomes just like the others in the Court. Gravelot
introduces himself to Valentín as the spirit of that Court, "the spirit of
evil" (G, 147). He wields power because he is intelligent and therefore can exploit the weaknesses of the others. He reveals to the
youthful and idealistic poet the meaning of the minuet. Under the
superficial beauty of the music and the dance lies a sordid reality:
"Some are ambitious. Others are traitors. Others have lost their
honor. But do you know what this group of people dancing before us
represents? These people, Valentín, represent Humanity" (G, 150).

Because people are hypocrites and morally weak themselves, it is
possible for the King's mistress and a cynical philosopher to rule the
country. This sceptical view of human nature is not far removed from
that underlying Benavente's *The Bonds of Interest*. We are turned
into puppets by our own defects of character. Holt sums up Ruiz
Iriarte's general position well when he points out that the playwright
is "a critical observer of hypocrisy and moral ambivalence in a sector
of contemporary society, and he has shown particular concern for the
sad destruction or compromise of ideals in a society that seems to
demand an unconscionable price if ambitions are to be fulfilled." [13]
Even if *The Grand Minuet* is set in the eighteenth century, Valentín's
loss of innocence and Gravelot's vicarious disillusionment could be
transposed to any other time or place in history.

The Grand Minuet stands apart from the rest of Ruiz Iriarte's theater in several ways.[14] It is his only play with a historical setting outside Spain and in fact is only one of a handful of plays that do not take place entirely in contemporary Madrid or nearby provincial cities.[15] With the minuet scene in the second act, it is the play requiring the most elaborate stage setting. But more significantly, it is the most pessimistic of Ruiz Iriarte's comedies and farces. The playwright may view human nature with a smile, but it is a smile tinged by sadness.

III   The Dinner of the Three Kings

Quite different in tone and intent is the third of the satirical farces, *La cena de los tres reyes* [The dinner of the three kings], which opened in Madrid in October, 1954. Probably because of its light-hearted quality, Marquerie called the play an operetta without music.[16] The scene is Christmas Eve at a mountain in in an unidentified country that might be Spain. Three deposed monarchs have agreed to meet there in secret to enjoy the holiday together. Two Russian spies, aware of the kings' plan, also arrive; they have been sent in accordance with a new Party line which calls for gaining control of the right by reestablishing monarchies. The other characters include a zany old Duchess who was herself a spy during World War I, a movie starlet, and the staff at the inn. As is true of most of Ruiz Iriarte's plays, *The Dinner of the Three Kings* evidences careful construction, clever dialogue, and a thorough knowledge of stock comic devices. Here he makes particular use of mistaken identities, comic reversals in attitude, and caricatures.

The Russian spies, though caricatures, do not both follow the same stereotyped image of a Communist that Alfonso Paso introduced to the Spanish stage a year before *The Dinner of the Three Kings* in his comedy *Una bomba llamada Abelardo* [A bomb named Abelard, 1953]. While Paso's Russian constantly preaches against capitalism, the younger of Ruiz Iriarte's spies is enchanted by everything he sees, including the cathedral. When all three kings reject the spies' offer to help them regain their thrones, Molinsky quickly decides to remain behind, too. As he explains to Koproff: "Because here there is no punishment, no sabotage, no Party. Because I am charmed by these people who are happy because they can do what they wish. Because I like girls who love one man for a lifetime . . . and because the Secret Service seems silly to me."[17] Koproff, realizing that he will be imprisoned if he returns to the Soviet Union alone, decides to defect.

Ruiz Iriarte pokes fun at the Communist spies, but he also aims his satire at the right and at those who view with nostalgia "the good old days." With the three kings he debunks a romanticized view of royalty. Alí-Harom, the deposed Arab king, is the most exaggerated of the three figures. Now he travels in an attention-getting "incognito" outfit and expects to be surrounded by photographers at all times. Still a rich man, he ultimately declines the Russian offer because he would rather continue to travel to the great capitals of Europe than stay home in his own country. The least comic of the three kings, Alberto was deposed in large part because his own idealistic, liberal policy encouraged his people to overthrow the monarchy. Now getting old and no longer wealthy, he has developed a much more sceptical outlook on life. For him the past is not worth recapturing. Not so cynical as Gravelot, he nevertheless believes that "saving humanity is a mania of young bachelors" (*K*, 81). Even farther removed from the traditional image of a king, however, is Prince Federico, pretender to the throne of his country. Shy and scholarly, while awaiting the time to become king, he studies. He rejects the spies' offer because he prefers being a free prince to a captive king. He assures the Russians that his decision is not prompted by an American offer: "Americans only need kings for Hollywood, and they make them up because they turn out better" (*K*, 93).

Federico is once again Ruiz Iriarte's *pobrecito*, and the romantic intrigue between him and Paloma, the movie starlet, is very similar to the main plots in several of the comedies of manners written during the same period. Paloma, in spite of her many love affairs, still dreams of Prince Charming. She is very disappointed when the mysterious prince at the inn turns out to be a timid and unassuming student. To win her love, Federico rents a princely uniform and cape from a theatrical costume shop and decides to fit himself into the stereotyped image she and his people have of a romantic and domineering monarch.

The satire in this farce is light and Ruiz Iriarte apparently has no serious message to express in it either with respect to political systems or human nature. While *A Day in Glory* and *The Grand Minuet* have been labeled "transcendental satires," [18] the same cannot be said of *The Dinner of the Three Kings*. Gonzalo Torrente Ballester was correct when he observed that Ruiz Iriarte might have attempted a more profound satire here but that instead he chose merely to entertain. [19]

CHAPTER 4

Role Playing and Role Reversal: The Comedies of Manners

IN analyzing the early plays of Ruiz Iriarte, Valbuena Prat observed that they could be divided into two periods: the works of poetic fantasy, culminating in *The Six-Horse Landau* and *The Grand Minuet*, and the subsequent comedies that, while continuing in an escapist vein, fell into a "clever formula." [1] Although Valbuena Prat criticized the second period for being "frivolous" and for including a series of plays all built on the same pattern, his reaction to the comedies was not totally negative: "Their art, their intent, their irony mark a type of comedy of excellent quality." Calling Ruiz Iriarte a modernized Benavente, Valbuena Prat found in the comedies, despite their formula, a reflection of the underlying anguish and problems of Spanish society in the mid-twentieth century.[2]

Valbuena Prat's identification of a series of plays built on a similar pattern is quite correct but the chronological division is not. The series actually begins with *El aprendiz de amante* [The apprentice lover] and *Las mujeres decentes* [Respectable women], both of which antedate the two plays he cities as the end of Ruiz Iriarte's first period. Schevill, who agrees with Valbuena Prat's thesis, identifies six comedies or farces containing the same dramatic formula: *The Apprentice Lover*, *Respectable Women*, *Juego de niños* [Child's play], *La soltera rebelde* [The rebellious spinster], *El pobrecito embustero* [The poor little liar], and *The Flowers Cafe*.[3] She finds that Ruiz Iriarte successfully blends the tragic concept of man's loneliness, insecurity and need for affection with the structure of comedy or farce. In some detail she defines the recurrent dramatic formula of the group. In each play there is a lonely individual who is honest and virtuous—what Schevill calls an authentic individual. But society places a greater value on glamour, aggressiveness and cleverness than on virtue or sincerity. The authentic individual is thus forced into creating a deception or withdrawing into his own poetic world in order to seek happiness. Eventually the authentic individual who has resorted to deception voluntarily rejects falsehood and returns to reality.

Although one may question the specific application of Schevill's formula to *The Flowers Cafe* in particular and, to a lesser extent, to *Respectable Women*, there is no doubt that Ruiz Iriarte has used a similar structure in several of his comedies. One or more characters in each of these plays will assume a role in order to achieve some sort of happiness or success. Typically the assumption of a new personality will lead to a role reversal: for example, the virtuous person will appear to be immoral. The role reversal allows the playwright to show us that society itself has an inverted system of values, for it is in the guise of the new personality that the individual gains recognition. Although Ruiz Iriarte does not adopt a moralizing tone neither does he have all of the comedies end on an equally happy note; his underlying message apparently is that true happiness can be achieved only through virtue and, as Schevill has noted, through acceptance of the authentic self.

Schevill astutely observes that the "authentic individual"—timid, honest, virtuous—may be either male or female and will accordingly be frequently contrasted with an aggressive, domineering female or a Don Juan figure. Pérez Minik and Baquero Goyanes have both identified the same recurrent figure, but only in the masculine *pobrecito* character.[4] Pérez Minik finds the character to be an attractive one with antecedents in the works of Cervantes, Galdós and Arniches, but considers the character's existence in the contemporary period to be surprising.[5] Baquero Goyanes elaborates on the subject, identifying the *pobrecito* as a key figure in *The Apprentice Lover*, *Cuando ella es la otra* [When she is the other woman], *Child's Play*, *The Rebellious Spinster*, and *The Poor Little Liar*.[6]

These plays, which have been grouped as a series either because of a common dramatic formula or the use of a repeated character, have been labeled by Ruiz Iriarte himself as comedies of manners, plays which reflect the customs of society at a given period of time.[7] It is a judgment with which critics generally agree. Pérez Minik, for example, has stated that Ruiz Iriarte's comedies are much closer to the reality of the moment than are the works of López Rubio or Neville and that his characters in general seem more familiar to his public.[8] Luis Molero Manglano, while suggesting that Ruiz Iriarte ignores the great passions and crises of life, nevertheless feels that his comedies are realistic because they deal with social customs which are in themselves realistic.[9] López Sancho finds that the plays, with their tendency to ignore the really harsh realities of life, capture very well the ideology of the Spanish middle-class in the postwar era. From his point of view these comedies of manners are not escapist either from the perspective of the playwright or from that of the audience. Ruiz Iriarte is not escaping from reality but rather is bearing witness to the spirit of the times. His audience does not escape because what they see on the stage is not someone else but themselves. Moreover, for López Sancho, Ruiz Iriarte's theater relates the changing standards and customs of Spanish society. [10]

While taken collectively the comedies of manners do not have the importance in Ruiz Iriarte's total theater either of his plays of poetic fantasy or of his later, somewhat more serious works of the 1960s, the group does include two of his most successful comedies: *The Apprentice Lover* and *Child's Play*. [11]

I   The Apprentice Lover

Following a première in Valencia in November, 1947, *El aprendiz de amante* [The apprentice lover] did not open in Madrid until April, 1949. The latter production, starring Carmen Carbonell and Antonio Vico, is considered by the playwright to be his first major commercial success and the real beginning of his professional career. [12] A carefully constructed farce, *The Apprentice Lover* introduces the typical pattern of Ruiz Iriarte's comedies of manners in plot, characterization, and structure. The basic story of the comedy is quite simple. Andrés, a shy, lonely young man from the provincial city of Burgos comes to Madrid where he falls in love with Catalina, a sophisticated and modern young woman who believes that a Don Juan would make an interesting and exciting husband. Andrés spreads the rumor that he is an unprincipled Romeo. Delighted with this false image, Catalina marries him only to discover on their wedding night that he is a virgin. Appalled that her reputation will be ruined, she both refuses to consummate the marriage and coerces him into pretending to be an unfaithful husband. After three unhappy months of playing the role of a Don Juan, Andrés says that Catalina is not his ideal of a woman anyway and decides to go home to Burgos alone. When Catalina learns that another woman has followed him there, she has a change of heart. She joins him in Burgos, declaring it to be the beginning of their honeymoon.

Andrés fulfills the definitions of the *pobrecito* discussed by Baquero Goyanes and of the authentic individual outlined by Schevill. He has neither the physical characteristics nor the personality of the romantic hero. In fact, Catalina tells him, before she learns the truth, that he is "the most dangerous kind of Don Juan. The kind who doesn't look like one!" [13] In appearance, she adds, he is "completely insignificant" (*AL*, 18). When Andrés finally confesses the truth about himself, he reveals that he was orphaned as a child, suffered from loneliness and sadness in his youth, and grew into a shy man. His only escape has been his imagination (*AL*, 21). In his poetic world, he had created the image of a perfect woman, calling her María Luisa. For him, Catalina is María Luisa come to life (*AL*, 23). After three months of pretending to be a Don Juan who deceives his wife, staying out almost every night in order to convince the maids and the neighbors that he has a series of mistresses, Andrés decides that he can play a false role no longer. Catalina is a "frivolous and stubborn doll," not his ideal María Luisa (*AL*, 47). In Schevill's terms, Andrés realizes that he must be true to his own inner authenticity. He therefore goes back to Burgos and to his poetic world where he belongs.

In Schevill's analysis of Ruiz Iriarte's dramatic formula, the foil to the *pobrecito* is a "cold, scheming, vain or prudish woman." [14] Catalina falls into this category, but like Andrés himself and many of the heroines in the plays of poetic fantasy she also has a vivid imagination. If Andrés had created an ideal "María Luisa" for himself, Catalina had also created an ideal spouse. While Andrés has been out at night circling the Plaza de la Independencia, half dead from the cold, Catalina has been home alone dreaming: "I dreamed that my husband was the most fascinating man in the world! That all women were envious of me!" (*AL*, 48). Andrés believes that true happiness can be found only in the simple and common things: wearing a comfortable dressing gown and sitting on the couch with one's little wife (*AL*, 49). But Catalina, in her fantasy, has dreamed of a marriage filled with adventure: "I was a woman who could only fall in love with the extraordinary. I was horrified by a common home with a common man" (*AL*, 25).

The success of *The Apprentice Lover* is dependent, however, not upon the plot or the contrast between the ideals of the two main characters but upon Ruiz Iriarte's skill as a writer of comedies and farces. The play opens in a hotel in El Escorial where the maids and the manager await the arrival of the newlyweds. The comic tone of the play, established by their conversation, is enhanced by the arrival of the nervous Andrés and the calm Catalina. Although the attitudes of the bride and groom would appear to be a role reversal, the manager assures Andrés that it is always the groom who is nervous. He is therefore not surprised that Andrés wants his suitcase in the bathroom, not the bedroom, and urges him to drink some champagne to prepare himself. Finally the newlyweds are left alone, and the comic tension increases. Exploiting the underlying humor of incongruity, Ruiz Iriarte has both bride and groom receive phone calls of inquiry on how the wedding night is going: one from Catalina's shy little sister and one from Andrés' cousin Germán.

By the middle of the first act when Catalina begins to recount Andrés' alleged amorous exploits, the groom is so well identified as a shy, nervous, innocent young man that the public is prepared for his confession. What is still unexpected and therefore comic when it occurs is Catalina's rejection of her husband. Although the basis of much of the humor in the wedding night scene and throughout the comedy is implicitly sexual, Ruiz Iriarte handles the topic with subtlety and tastefulness. Pérez Minik has observed that he was the only playwright in Spain to dare to touch such themes in the period.[15] To varying degrees, all of his comedies of manners deal with adultery, illicit love affairs, and sexual relations; it is undoubtedly for this reason that his works are often compared to the French "boulevard" comedies.[16]

At the close of act one, Ruiz Iriarte develops a high level of expectation on the part of the audience. The differences between Catalina and Andrés would appear to be irreconcilable. It is not clear what possibly can happen next. The scene of the second act is the apartment of the young couple. Catalina is home alone, accompanied by her maids and her next-door neighbor, Gaby, all of whom are apparently scandalized by Andrés' love affairs. Building on the humor of incongruity emanating from an inverted value system, Ruiz Iriarte has Catalina not only express satisfaction at Andrés' conduct but comfort Gaby that she need not worry, that her husband will deceive her too. There is a comic irony throughout the act because the audience is now in on the secret. When the weary Andrés finally appears, there takes place a delightful conversation filled with double meanings between him and Gaby. Ultimately we learn that Gaby, the maids, and perhaps all Madrid love Andrés for being an unprincipled and therefore irresistible lover. Like George Bernard Shaw in *Man and Superman* (1903), Ruiz Iriarte plays with the Don Juan myth and suggests that the women are the real aggressors. He also satirizes a society that finds immorality more interesting than fidelity while simultaneously exploiting to the fullest the comic irony that Andrés' reputation is not deserved. Andrés is the exact opposite of the traditional hypocrite who appears to be good but is not, and Catalina's reaction when he abandons her is a comic deformation of the traditional desire to defend oneself against what people will say. The resourceful and imaginative woman spreads the rumor that her husband has run off with a princess.

In several of his plays, Ruiz Iriarte develops a comic contrast between life in the city—Madrid—and life in the provinces. This is partially the basis of the humor in the third act, set in Andrés' old family home in Burgos. His two elderly servants are caricatures. Felisa, who has worked for the family for fifty years, is a spinster and therefore must be sheltered from the details about Andrés' supposed conduct. Both servants are horrified at what will happen to their reputations now that the "truth" about their master's life in Madrid is known. Andrés has gone home looking for peace, but the servants think he is lying. They even believe that he is hiding the princess somewhere.

The climax of the play comes with the arrival of an unknown woman who claims to be María Luisa. She is Germán's mistress Manolita who has learned from him the story of Andrés' true character and of his deception. Tired of a life in which she has gone from one lover to another, she has been attracted to a man who could be faithful to one woman. Andrés rejects her because he really loves Catalina, but Catalina, who has come to Burgos in pursuit of Manolita, learns from her the true value of her husband. It is because of Manolita's wise advice that Catalina decides to stay with Andrés and become his ideal. Like Paulina in *Academy of Love*, Manolita uses her own bitter experiences to help another woman find marital happiness.[17]

The Apprentice Lover is generally a well made comedy. The action moves forward at a rapid pace, with comic situation built upon comic situation. Its major structural flaw is the ending, where Manolita's intervention and Catalina's change of heart both seem contrived. However, the overall tone of the play is that of farce, and in farce implausible endings are not so unacceptable as in serious drama. Certainly the initial success of the comedy would indicate that the Spanish public was content with the happy ending. The target of Ruiz Iriarte's gentle satire here, as in his other comedies of manners, is post Civil War Madrid. In spite of the size of the city, it is actually a closed society where gossip travels fast. As Andrés tells Catalina: "In Madrid you can get the reputation of a scoundrel in a couple of days and it will last your whole life" (*AL*, 22). Catalina invents love affairs for her husband and writes them in her private diary, knowing full well that the maids will snoop in her room and then spread the stories. But most important, Ruiz Iriarte here as elsewhere is examining changing moral values and the changing role of women in Spanish society.

II   Respectable Women

The propensity toward gossip and the inverted moral values of modern society are similarly the objects of Ruiz Iriarte's satire in his next comedy of manners *Las mujeres decentes* [Respectable women]. The farce, which opened in Barcelona in June, 1949, and in Madrid in September of the same year, is, however, more complex in its plot and structure than *The Apprentice Lover*. The main character, Paulina, is a feminine counterpart of Andrés. Virtuous, shy, and imaginative, she has written three novels but has failed to achieve fame. Her uncle, Don Fabián, suggests that her problem is that she is too respectable. Following his hint, she spreads a rumor that she is the mistress of a certain Jerónimo. The novel in which she reveals the details of their imaginary affair makes her an international celebrity. On her return from a triumphant visit to Hollywood, reporters learn that a real Jerónimo, a humble taxi driver, exists. Fearful that this revelation will destroy her career, Paulina attempts to hire Jerónimo to pretend to be her lover. Jerónimo, who is really an impoverished aristocrat in love with Paulina, sets as a condition that she marry him and then promises to pursue the career for which he was trained.

The Paulina story is very close to that of Andrés in *The Apprentice Lover*. As a *pobrecita*, Paulina is doomed to failure. Once society believes her to be immoral, her success is assured. As Schevill has observed, "the unsavory reputation created by the novel makes her the glamorous idol of the same public that had rejected her before." Ironically, the scandalous love affair of her latest novel is no less fiction than were the plots of her other works. It is a Pirandellian situation in which, for the public and the literary critics, appearance is more important than reality. But Paulina does not completely fit into the dramatic formula outlined by Schevill. She does not voluntarily reject falsehood in order to return to her authentic role and in fact attempts to circumvent the truth when it is revealed by Jerónimo.

Nor is Jerónimo as timid and virtuous as both Schevill and Morales suggest.[19] Until he had lost his fortune, he had been something of a playboy. It is only in his role as a cab driver that he assumes a humble aspect. He is accompanied in his new life by his dignified servant, Domingo, who, in his impeccable manners and plain common sense, is reminiscent of similar servants in the plays of Shaw and other British playwrights. Because Jerónimo is to a large extent a caricature of the idle rich it is therefore not surprising that Domingo has to remind him at the end what the career was that he had prepared in his university studies.

Interwoven with the Paulina-Jerónimo story and thus complicating the farce is a subplot relating to Paloma, the victim of an errant husband. As if she were following the advice of Madame Fleriot in *Academy of Love*, she resorts to theatrical efforts to win back the affection of her spouse. She pretends to abandon him, then to make him jealous makes up the story that she has become the imaginary Jerónimo's mistress during Paulina's trip to Hollywood, and finally tries at the conclusion of the play to pay the real Jerónimo to play the role of her lover. While the Paulina-Jerónimo story has an apparent happy ending, Paloma's marital problems remain unresolved.

As in the other comedies of manners, role playing and role reversal form essential elements of the plot. Paulina and Paloma, the respectable women, attempt to appear sexually liberated in order to achieve success or happiness. Jerónimo, the aristocrat, assumes the role of a working man. But in *Respectable Women*, as in the plays of poetic fantasy, Ruiz Iriarte also develops extensively the theme of illusion versus reality. Paulina knows that a real Jerónimo exists—she has found his suitcase in a hotel room with autographed pictures from three women and a copy of one of her own novels—but she believes that she has never seen him. The Jerónimo she creates in her own mind and in her novel is strictly imaginary. In this respect she is like the Isabels of *Suicide Bridge* and *The Six-Horse Landau* or like Andrés in *The Apprentice Lover* in her ability to fall in love with an illusion. Paulina's illusion, however, has more vitality than do these other imaginary loves, for other characters also begin to believe in Jerónimo. Paloma falls in love with her version of Jerónimo, and even Remedios, Paulina's housekeeper and the only person in on the secret, finds that she imagines herself having an affair with him. The fictitious Jerónimo begins to have a real and potentially destructive impact on the lives of several characters similar to the equally imaginary title character of López Rubio's *Alberto*, a play also staged in 1949.

Ruiz Iriarte labels *Respectable Women* a farce and indeed does structure the play accordingly. The first act, like the first act of *The Apprentice Lover*, takes place in a provincial hotel. This one is advertised as a "marvelous place of rest between the sea and the mountain." [20] The hotel, however, is so far between the sea and the mountain that neither is readily accessible; the "peace" is greatly restricted by the dance band and by a child who plays the drum in the corridors. The stage setting itself shows the corridor and two identical rooms, the one Paloma checks into and the one erroneously assigned to both Jerónimo and Paulina. The audience knows long before either Jerónimo or Paulina does that the management has made the error and can anticipate the inevitable confrontation when its discovery is made. By the time Jerónimo walks in on Paulina, who is already retired for the night, she has invented her ideal Jerónimo. The real Jerónimo, realizing that he does not fit that image, lies, saying that he is his own servant come to claim the suitcase. This deception sets the stage for an obligatory scene in which Paulina will learn his true identity.

In the second act, when Jerónimo himself appears as the cab driver who has brought Paulina home from the airport, Ruiz Iriarte continues to build a farcical situation on the basis of the mistaken identity. Much to the amusement of Paulina, her visitors, and the reporters, the cab driver announces that he reads and rereads her novel in order to get to know himself better; Domingo adds that Jerónimo even dreams that he is Jerónimo. It is when Paloma reveals that she has become Jerónimo's mistress during Paulina's absence that Jerónimo is forced to identify himself. Paulina, in her anger, suggests that Paloma's husband has every right to kill Jerónimo. Jerónimo in comic fear protests his innocence.

In the third act, the playwright develops further the inverted moral values of contemporary society. Paulina and Remedios are disgraced now that everyone knows that Paulina is respectable. Even her conservative Uncle Fabián is displeased because his niece's scandalous life had made him a social success. The conclusion also exploits the comic potential in the reversion of Paulina and Jerónimo to their true characters. Paulina, the alleged woman of the world, is horrified when Jerónimo asks to kiss her. Finally, Jerónimo, after proposing marriage, doffs his cabbie's uniform and emerges as the well dressed aristocrat he initially was. The ending is contrived—like that of *The Apprentice Lover*—but acceptable within the context of farce.

III   When She Is the Other Woman

The changing role of women in Spanish society, a subject which underlies Ruiz Iriarte's comedies of manners, has attracted his attention in his newspaper articles as well. In *"Los maridos han cambiado mucho"* [Husbands have changed a lot], he indicates that it is actually women who have changed.[21] Docile wives no longer patiently sit at home pretending to ignore their husbands' infidelity. Far more sophisticated and less restricted to their homes than Spanish women of earlier generations, the modern Spanish wife simply will not allow her husband to abandon her. Several Spanish playwrights have used the contrast between the traditional, conservative Spanish woman and her liberated, Americanized counterpart as the basis for comedies.[22] Nowhere is this comic contrast developed more extensively than in Ruiz Iriarte's *Cuando ella es la otra* [When she is the other woman] in which he reverses roles and has the wife be modern and liberal and the mistress be the conservative, "respectable" woman.

When She Is the Other Woman opened in Barcelona in February, 1951, and in Madrid in April, 1952. Both productions starred Carmen Carbonell and Antonio Vico, the same actors who created the lead roles in *The Apprentice Lover*. Although it is not one of Ruiz Iriarte's best comedies, it was highly praised by Joaquín de Entrambasaguas, and a less enthusiastic Torrente Ballester noted nevertheless that it was an ingenious work marked by its sparkling dialogue.[23] Baquero Goyanes, who includes the play in the group featuring the *pobrecito* figure, similarly finds the farce to be clever, original, and funny.[24]

The play opens in the oldfashioned apartment of Patricia, a kept woman who is preparing to leave on a trip with her latest lover, Gabriel. Patricia, in the opening dialogue and throughout the play, insists that she is very respectable and deplores the lack of morality in modern society. The inversion of values is reinforced by her maids who agree that they never knew what a decent home was like until they came to work for Patricia. Gabriel arrives, visibly nervous. Finally he admits that his wife has come along. Verónica, who is as modern as Patricia is conservative, greets her husband's mistress warmly, offers her friendly advice, and finally promises to be like a mother to her. Rather than viewing a fight as he had expected, Gabriel finds the two women siding against him in a discussion. Gabriel is confused by what transpires; his discomfiture and Verónica's incongruous attitude form the basis of the comic effect of the scene.

The scene is interrupted by the unexpected arrival of the middle-aged Bobby, Patricia's most recent former lover, who still has a key to the apartment. The women leave to prepare cocktails and the two men, in a comic repetition of the conversation in which Patricia and Verónica established their surprising relationship, find that they, too, can be friends. As Bobby explains, "We men really like one another when we agree on something, when we have the same tastes." [25]

Continuing with his technique of building farcical situations on inverted values, Ruiz Iriarte uses this cliché to suggest that two men who share a mistress will naturally have much in common. The act ends with Verónica's disclosure that Patricia, who is not used to alcoholic beverages, has become intoxicated from sampling the cocktails in the kitchen and, unfortunately, will not be able to go away with Gabriel after all.

Acts two and three take place in Verónica and Gabriel's home. Verónica is preparing to go out with Bobby, much to the amazement of her butler. Bobby, however, is not amazed. By the middle of the second act, when he calls Verónica's bluff, we are able to see the true wife behind the role she has been playing. Verónica really loves Gabriel even though their marriage has been ten years of constant bickering, and she has resorted to her farcical friendship with his mistress as a last effort to keep him from leaving her. Bobby joins in the pretense. With his help, Gabriel, made to feel jealous, is finally seduced by his own wife, who for the night becomes "the other woman" herself. Patricia is so scandalized when she finds that Gabriel has betrayed her with "her best friend" that she calls him names and walks out on him. Bobby, who says that he would like to settle down at last under the guise of respectability and be called Don Roberto, decides to marry Patricia and move to the provinces. Verónica and Gabriel are reunited.

Though *When She Is the Other Woman* is light comedy, Ruiz Iriarte does not provide a traditional happy ending. Verónica, who had been a conservative young wife, had deliberately assumed the role of a "modern" woman—one who races sports cars, cheats at bridge, smokes and drinks—because Gabriel had been attracted by such women. Now that he is attracted by conservative women, she is willing to adopt that role instead. She will no longer treat Gabriel like a *pobrecito* and he will dominate the marriage. The result is a comic scene of indecision and boredom. After several minutes even Gabriel has to admit that the domineering, proud woman was more charming than the docile slave and begs her to call him *pobrecito* once again. The ending is thus ambiguous. Gabriel and Verónica are back where they started with no solution to their marital conflicts. In this respect the ending is like that of Federico García Lorca's farce *La zapatera prodigiosa* [The shoemaker's prodigious wife, 1930] in which the happily reunited couple begin to fight as always. Friction between husband and wife is a stock situation in farce, and one could cite many other similar examples; but in the case of Ruiz Iriarte, there may occur the more serious suggestion that marital happiness in modern society is difficult, if not impossible. In several of his plays, both comic and serious, his view of marriage appears to be pessimistic. If the wife is traditional and subservient, her husband probably is unfaithful to her. If she is modern and more aggressive, she is caught between the moral code with which she was raised and the changing attitudes of society, and her husband may be unfaithful anyway. In *Academy of Love* Madame Fleriot finds the cure for sick marriages, but in the plays dealing with particular marriages in depth, the marital relation is seldom healthy. Valbuena Prat was quite correct in noting that the basic situation of *When She Is the Other Woman* and the comedy that followed, *Child's Play*, was the same even though the wife in the former is strong and aggressive while the wife in the latter is weak and loving.[26]

IV Child's Play

Juego de niños [Child's play] is the best known of Ruiz Iriarte's comedies of manners and one of his most successful plays. The playwright dedicated the comedy to Tina Gascó, who starred in the production opening in Madrid in January, 1952. The play subsequently won the National Theater Prize for that year. Translated into German and Portuguese, it has been performed in various countries. In 1954 it was staged simultaneously in Lisbon, Mexico City, and Santiago de Chile,[28] and three years later was made into a movie starring Ana Mariscal, Jorge Rigaud, and Juan José Menéndez.[29] Critics at the time felt that it represented a synthesis of Ruiz Iriarte's best theatrical techniques and the zenith of his mature works.[30]

Once again role playing and role reversal form the basic elements of the plot. Ricardo is a philandering husband who frequently stays out all night. His wife Cándida loves him deeply and is hurt by his infidelity but in front of their teenage sons Tony and Manolín and their teenage niece Maité pretends that she either does not understand what he is doing or is not humiliated by his actions. He, in turn, attempts to lie to both her and the children about his activities. But the three young people are too sophisticated to accept lies and pretense. In a clever role reversal, Ruiz Iriarte has the children scold

Ricardo and attempt to raise him properly. Led by Maité, they also decide to help Cándida solve her marital problems.

As in *When She Is the Other Woman*, Ruiz Iriarte juxtaposes the traditional woman and the modern one. In this case, it is the youthful Maité who stands in contrast to the oldfashioned Cándida. She assures her aunt that the only way to win and hold Ricardo's affection is through jealousy. She then also decides that the ideal man to play the role of Cándida's lover is Marcelo Duval, Maité's French teacher. Timid, idealistic and charming, Marcelo is the *pobrecito* figure. For Baquero Goyanes he is "one of the best-developed characters in Spanish comedy of recent years" and, by himself, "enough to justify the whole work." [31] Although his "courtship" of Cándida is purely platonic—much to her dismay they spend their time visiting the tourist attractions that a good Spaniard studiously avoids—and he never openly declares his love outside the context of the game they are playing. Cándida knows, however, as does the audience, that Marcelo's affection is real. She undoubtedly is speaking the truth when she tells Ricardo that underneath the timid exterior, Marcelo is a passionate man, one who would be an ideal husband. It is Ricardo who is not suited for marriage and would be the ideal lover. [32] Cándida's conclusion expresses not only another example of role reversal in the comedy but repeats the apparent position of the author with respect to the *pobrecito* and similar characters throughout these early comedies. We should judge people by their inner worth and not by their external characteristics. The shy and less glamorous person though maybe not so attractive to the opposite sex as are the Ricardos of the world may yet prove to be more capable of genuine love. Although Ruiz Iriarte's comedies of manners are not overtly moralistic, their implicit message is that society has erroneously sacrificed sincerity for superficiality.

As a traditional Spanish wife, Cándida initially rejects Maité's suggestion for winning back her husband. She abhors the idea of a "modern" marriage in which wives flirt with their husbands' friends, go to parties and nightclubs. "You want to turn me into one of those wives who lead the same lives with their husbands now that husbands used to live with their mistresses," she tells Maité in horror (*J*, 24). Nevertheless, she agrees to participate in the game Maité proposes. What begins as child's play, a simple and easy children's game, comes dangerously close to becoming reality. After Marcelo has declared his love for Cándida in front of an increasingly jealous and irate Ricardo, Cándida tells her husband that sometimes an adult game may begin as child's play (*J*, 50). In the role she plays for her husband's benefit, she accepts Marcelo's truth over Ricardo's infidelity, but the role and the reality of Cándida have begun to merge. At the end of the play, when Marcelo has forced Ricardo into expressing his love for his wife and his children have told him that he need suffer no more because the Marcelo-Cándida affair is fiction, Cándida is saddened by the loss of Marcelo and his loyal affection. She warns Maité against running the risk of ever entering into such a pretense of love: "I was in on the joke and I knew it was all a game. But, at the same time, I was a poor woman living a great adventure for the first time. . . . . It's best to live taking what life gives us. Laughter or tears. But without playing" (*J*, 69).

Ruiz Iriarte says in his self-criticism of *Child's Play* that it is a happy, optimistic comedy.[33] But his assessment is not totally accurate. Underneath the happy ending is an undercurrent of sadness. There is no reason to believe that Ricardo has really reformed. In fact, the final scene indicates his intense interest in the potential love lives of his two sons: Tony, who is pursued by emancipated young girls, including Maité, and Manolín, the chip off the old block, who chases the maid. The self-effacing Marcelo, who has sacrificed himself to Cándida's theoretical happiness, is gone for good. For Cándida herself, there are no alternatives to her present situation. She has apparently married the wrong man; but in Spain there is no solution to that problem for an honorable, religious woman.

Like the other comedies of manners, *Child's Play* utilizes the structure and, to some extent, the characters of farce. Torrente Ballester, in fact, has stated that the technique of the play reminds him of an animated cartoon in which a couple of real actors intervene.[34] Although most of the characters are treated as caricatures, including Ricardo, Cándida and Marcelo are human beings, capable of feeling the anguish of loneliness and the warmth of friendship and love. Schevill finds that the play achieves a perfect balance between comedy and tragedy.[35] *Child's Play*, an excellent example of the repeated dramatic formula Schevill has outlined in her analysis of Ruiz Iriarte's theater, is, she says, in the group a typical comedy. Cándida is the authentic person, sincere and virtuous, who is forced into assuming a role quite foreign to her own upbringing in order to win back the love of her frivolous husband. She voluntarily rejects the false image both because she has ostensibly achieved her goal and because she realizes that the game could be dangerous. In giving her advice to Maité, she returns their relationship to the normal one—

the adult giving direction to the teenager—and indicates that it is better to be true to one's own self, even if the result is tears, than to build happiness on a false precept. It is essentially the same moral choice Lupe will make at the conclusion of *The Rebellious Spinster*.

V   The Rebellious Spinster

Child's Play premièred in Madrid in January, 1952; *La soltera rebelde* [The rebellious spinster] opened the same year at the beginning of the fall theatrical season with almost exactly the same cast. Tina Gascó, who had played Laura in *The Flowers Cafe* and Cándida in *Child's Play*, starred in the title role of Lupe. Carlos Casaravilla, who had created the bohemian artist César in *The Flowers Cafe* and the French tutor Marcelo in *Child's Play*, was cast as Esteban, a bohemian organist and another in the series of *pobrecitos*. Victoria Rodríguez, who had been Cris and Maité in the earlier plays, appeared as Maty, one of Lupe's two modern young nieces, and the same actors who portrayed Cándida's sons took the roles of the nieces' boyfriends in *The Rebellious Spinster*. Torrente Ballester, while recognizing certain theatrical values in Ruiz Iriarte's latest comedy, noted at the time that *The Rebellious Spinster* reflected a formula that the playwright had begun to handle with such ease that he could turn out countless comedies, all entertaining but superficial, by merely following the same recipe.[36] Quite obviously part of the repetition in character and situation may be attributed to the fact that Ruiz Iriarte was writing these plays in rapid succession with particular actors in mind for the roles.[37]

The principal plot of *The Rebellious Spinster* is somewhat different from that of the comedies of manners in general although certain secondary characters and situations are repeated ones. Lupe, an attractive woman in her thirties, has lived a secluded life in the provincial city Montalbán. She has remained single in part because of her reputation for a bad temper and in part because of a fear of physical contact with men. Her frivolous sister Adelaida, a wealthy widow with two college-age daughters, has decided to bring Lupe to Madrid and marry her off in order to please her own vanity. As the play begins, Lupe is terrorizing the family and the maids with a violent display of temper on the eve of her wedding. Finally she reveals to the nieces, who are as emancipated and sophisticated as Maité in the previous comedy, that she had been repelled by Joaquín, her fiancé, when he had attempted to kiss her the night before.

Mónica, the older and more scholarly of the two young women, diagnoses her aunt's problem as a complex she developed as a child when the family administrator had tried to kiss her. Much to Adelaida's dismay, Lupe calls off the wedding. Lupe then disappears from her sister's home and spends several days wandering the streets of Madrid, dressed in stylish new clothes, in an effort to have some other man try to kiss her. She is now curious as to whether all men repel her or only Joaquín. Unsuccessful in this effort—Madrid is not as dangerous a place as people in the provinces believe—she returns to her sister's home and, with the help of the nieces, begins to date the humble but charming organist, Esteban. Like Marcelo in *Child's Play* under similar circumstances, Esteban had noticed Lupe before and was already attracted to her. He willingly escorts her to his favorite places and apparently loves her. Finally he kisses her one night in the elevator and she finds the experience pleasurable. But she decides that the time is already past for her to love and voluntarily returns alone to Montalbán and her private, secluded life.

As in *Child's Play*, Ruiz Iriarte develops a contrast between the two generations. The nieces, Mónica and Maty, and Joaquín's sons, Jaime and Pepito, are all modern young people; to some extent, their relationship to their elders represents a role reversal. Joaquín, another *pobrecito* figure, is a widower whose sons have tried to arrange a marriage for him. Mónica and Maty are not only more sophisticated than their aunt but better prepared than their mother to explain the facts of life to Lupe on the eve of her wedding day. Maty is very similar in character to Maité. It is she who pursues the studious Jaime. Mónica, however, is more interested in books than in men. In one comic scene Adelaida is greatly upset that Maty spends all her time looking in the mirror while Mónica spends all of hers with her nose buried in a book. She takes Mónica's book and gives it to Maty and Maty's mirror to give to Mónica. But it is Aunt Lupe who succeeds in changing Mónica. At the end of the play, when she has learned the truth about herself, she has also discovered that Mónica's interest in learning is a defense against her sister's greater popularity. Lupe advises Mónica to give up her studies, marry and have children so that she will not be a spinster like her aunt.[38] Mónica takes her aunt's advice and begins to flirt with Pepito, Jaime's athletic younger brother.

Wade considers *The Rebellious Spinster* to be a well structured play that "makes excellent sense psychologically."[39] However a careful analysis of the comedy does not justify this praise. Lupe is too

complex a character to be a comic figure but not well enough developed or consistent to convince us she is a real human being. Her
bad temper seems more a comic device than a necessary part of her
personality; also her decision to return home is inconsistent either
with her willingness to walk the streets of Madrid looking for men or
her obvious enjoyment of Esteban's company. Since it is less apparent here than in the previous comedies that Lupe has merely
assumed a false role to achieve some purpose, it is even less clear that
the conclusion, with its apparent sacrifice, represents a necessary
return to her authentic self. Moreover it is difficult to understand why
Joaquín, who is very similar in personality to Esteban and quite
charming in his shy way, repels Lupe while the organist does not. Not
only is the ending contrived as is the case in some of the other farces,
but the characters and situations themselves seem to have been
forced to fit a particular mold with somewhat unsatisfactory results.

VI The Poor Little Liar

Superior to *The Rebellious Spinster* and among the best of the
comedies of manners is *El pobrecito embustero* [The poor little liar],
which opened in April, 1953, and starred Carmen Carbonell and
Antonio Vico. While the farce is structured on the familiar dramatic
formula outlined by Schevill, it is also somewhat related both to Ruiz
Iriarte's plays of poetic fantasy in its use of an illusion-reality theme
and to his satirical works.[40] *The Poor Little Liar* and *Child's Play* are
the only two of Ruiz Iriarte's comedies of manners to have been
chosen by Sainz de Robles as among the outstanding plays of their
respective theatrical seasons.[41] While Holt considers the later comedy to be a "less polished piece of dramatic writing" than *Child's
Play*,[42] Fernández Cuenca feels that *The Poor Little Liar* was the
most thoughtful, the most inspired and the most important of Ruiz
Iriarte's plays up to that time.[43] He also indicates, as did Rodríguez
de León in his review, that Ruiz Iriarte's approach to farce, with its
undercurrent of tragic implications, resembles the tragicomedy of
Arniches. For the latter critic the blend of tragedy and comedy in
Ruiz Iriarte's plays is what distinguishes it from French farces like
those of André Roussin, which tend more toward the facile and
somewhat risqué humor of the boulevard or vaudeville theater.[44]
This is a judgment with which the playwright himself would doubt-
less agree. Iriarte has stated that the perfect expression of a theater of
humor is tragicomedy.[45]

Lorenzo, the *pobrecito* of the title, is a shy, scholarly man. Ridiculed by his students at the girls' school where he teaches, unloved by his wife Rosalía, unrecognized for his research by the academic world, he has taken refuge in his books. His one last hope of being understood by someone rests with the arrival from Mexico of his teenage nephew Pedrín. When that hope, too, is dashed, he begins to envy the lot of another man in the provincial town who because he is dying is the recipient of his family's undivided attention and love. Lorenzo tells his friend, the doctor Don Julián, that he would give anything for such a month of happiness. When the maid misinterprets something Lorenzo says and the rumor spreads that it is he who is dying, he conceals the truth in order to enjoy the affection and respect that are suddenly showered upon him. Ultimately he reveals the truth of his good health, in spite of the animosity that he can anticipate from the townspeople when they learn of his deception, because he discovers that Pedrín and Loreto, one of his students, really do love him and suffer because they believe him to be dying. Lorenzo's situation reverts to that of the beginning of the play before he adopted the role of a terminally ill person. But when he is hit by an automobile, Rosalía realizes his true worth, and the play ends happily.

Lorenzo's deception is not the only one in the play. Rosalía, like the wife in *The Apprentice Lover*, is an imaginative woman who has in her own mind created an ideal husband. Jealous of her sister Victoria who was always prettier and luckier, she has conveyed this false image to her in letters to Mexico. The fictitious Lorenzo, the one Pedrín expects to meet upon his arrival, is a dashing army officer, not a humble schoolteacher. But Victoria, too, has been guilty of inventing an illusion to replace an unacceptable reality. To Rosalía and Magdalena, their unmarried sister who lives with Rosalía and Lorenzo, she writes of the excitement and happiness she and her wealthy husband enjoy together. Pedrín however, eventually reveals to Loreto that his father is unfaithful to his mother and that his mother is so wrapped up in her drinking, her socializing, and her possessions that she doesn't seem to care. Before the news arrives that his parents are getting divorced, he has already told his new friend that he never wants to go home. Rosalía's marriage, not so superficially glamorous as that of Victoria, has had a greater potential for genuine happiness.

This is a conclusion which Magdalena reinforces when she drops the mask she wears. If she has been a deeply religious woman, spending all her time at mass and in church activities, it has been a role she has adopted because she had no alternative:

I was the good sister, the insignificant one, the *pobrecita*, who listened wide-eyed to your marvelous fantasies. Because I dreamed, too, you know. But my dreams would have made you two laugh. I dreamed humble, simple adventures, those that really happen in life. You understand? A husband, children. This house . . . I would not have known how to make up another husband, I would have really loved my husband. Mine. I, are you listening, Rosalía? I would have been very happy with a man like Lorenzo. And I would be proud to be his wife.[46]

The failure of Victoria's marriage and Magdalena's confession prepare Rosalía for her change of heart toward Lorenzo at the end of the play.

As is typical in Ruiz Iriarte's comedies of manners, these serious themes in *The Poor Little Liar* are presented within the structure of farce. Act one begins with the arrival of Pedrín. Rosalía tells Magdalena of the false Lorenzo she has created over the years, thus allowing us to anticipate an obligatory comic scene in which Pedrín and Lorenzo meet one another. The act ends with Lorenzo's unintentional lie about his dying, which provokes a comic reversal in the attitude of the others toward him. The reversal itself allows for a comic inversion of values, a technique frequently used by Ruiz Iriarte. Because Lorenzo is now honored rather than ridiculed, Rosalía is congratulated on his dying. In the third act, with the inevitable reversal resulting from learning the truth about Lorenzo's health, the inversion of values continues as Rosalía is offered sympathy on her husband's survival. When Lorenzo really is hit by an automobile, the repetition of his claim of being sick is met by a reaction opposite to that in the first act. The maids, Magdalena, and even Pedrín and Loreto, who earlier accepted falsehood as truth, now reject the truth as falsehood. Throughout the farce the playwright exploits to the fullest the comic irony in these situations.

Ruiz Iriarte's intention in *The Poor Little Liar* is satirical, and the object of his satire is not limited to Lorenzo's immediate family and acquaintances. As a modest and unassuming person, he is not appreciated by his wife; but as a serious scholar, he is not appreciated by society as a whole. It is only with his impending death that people begin to read his books, that Villanueva intends to honor him with a statue, that the governor of the province comes to pay him tribute, and that the Royal Academy plans to nominate him for membership. As Lorenzo remarks about fame and glory, "What a shame that all this is not for the living!" (*P*, 343). Ruiz Iriarte extends his satire to the publicity conscious heroes and heroines of popular culture through a movie star who comes to have her picture taken with the dying

Lorenzo. Needless to say, she is indignant when he does not die on schedule. Torrente Ballester feels that the introduction of this latter character is a serious defect in the play.[47] Certainly she only belongs if we view the play as a broad satire of contemporary society. The theme here is very similar to the one in *A Day in Glory*. Linda Martín has portrayed Queen Isabel, although she does not resemble her at all. Historical figures, to have popular commercial appeal, must fit a "Hollywood" image, and fame is reserved for the handsome and the beautiful,—however vacuous—rather than for the brave or the intelligent. Once again, Ruiz Iriarte is depicting a culture scornful of genuine worth that places a false emphasis on superficial glamour.

Perhaps less necessary to the development of the play than the inclusion of the movie star is the overt and somewhat repeated presentation of the moral behind the story. Lorenzo justifies the lie of his impending death to Don Julián by pointing out that "death is the only certain truth in our lives" (*P*, 334). He later explains that we show affection for the dying person because of our "fear and remorse for having not previously loved him as much as we should have loved him" (*P*, 349). His obvious conclusion, in the closing lines of the play, is that we should express our love every hour of every day, because in truth death is always near and what we all live for is a bit of warmth and affection (*P*, 358). In general Ruiz Iriarte is not overly moralistic in his comedies; but in this case he has directly expressed the message we are to find underneath the farce.

VII   You're Not Dangerous

Superficially similar in pattern to the other comedies of manners, *Usted no es peligrosa* [You're not dangerous] lacks the undercurrent of tragedy found in the best of the plays in this group and presents no well developed characters. Although it is clearly not one of Ruiz Iriarte's more important works, Torrente Ballester has found the play to be well constructed and the dialogue both witty and natural.[48] Starring Isabel Garcés, the same actress who created the related character of Paulina in *Respectable Women*, *You're Not Dangerous* opened in Madrid in October, 1954.

Marta, a *pobrecita* figure, is secretly in love with her next-door neighbor Fernando, a novelist with a reputation as a lover. As the play opens, he has sent for three of his exmistresses to see if one of them will play the role of his wife while they visit his rich, elderly, ill uncle in Valladolid who thinks that Fernando is married. None of the three is willing, but Fernando's maid, who knows of Marta's love, arranges for her to go. The second act takes place in Valladolid with the inevitable farcical scene in which the virtuous Marta finds herself spending the night in the same bedroom with her alleged husband. Much to her dismay, however, he merely falls asleep. Humiliated that she is not "dangerous," she spreads the rumor on their return to Madrid that he did, in fact, take advantage of her. The maid, the neighbors, and the exgirlfriends try to force Fernando into agreeing to marry Marta in order to restore her honor. But Marta herself has insured that the marriage will take place. She has told Fernando's uncle that they were not ever married but has promised him that they will marry. Fernando, who is counting on the inheritance from his uncle, really has no choice.

In developing his comedy, Ruiz Iriarte uses a number of the techniques, situations, and characters we have seen in his other plays. Fernando's guests in the first act arrive one by one, like the Duke's guests in *The Six-Horse Landau*; similarly the first two guests greet each other antagonistically. The third woman does not come; instead her husband arrives as her representative. Like Bobby with his unexpected attitude toward Gabriel in *When She Is the Other Woman*, Primitivo surprises us by regarding Fernando a friend rather than a rival. Ruiz Iriarte exploits the comic contrast between the provincial Valladolid and the more liberal atmosphere of Madrid. Although Pepita, a student who changes her field of study with each new lover, does not worry about her reputation in the capital city, she would not go to Valladolid with Fernando unless they were really married. The servant who greets Fernando and Marta at the uncle's home is very old, like the servants in *The Six-Horse Landau* or *The Apprentice Lover*, and a comic character. His nickname is Chico, "the Kid," and he cheats at cards. The cardgame itself, which is a device on the part of Fernando and Marta to keep Chico from leaving them alone, is reminiscent of the first act of *The Apprentice Lover* when the groom tries to keep the hotel manager in the room with him and his bride. *You're Not Dangerous* is a fast moving, funny play, but basically superficial, more open to the charge of being mere entertainment or vaudeville than most of the playwright's other works.

VIII   The Private Life of Mama

Also among Ruiz Iriarte's less important works and the last of the plays we have grouped as comedies of manners is *La vida privada de mamá* [The private life of mama], which starred Tina Gascó and opened in Madrid in October, 1956. Wade has called it "a sort of naughty bedroom farce" and Pérez Minik finds it surprisingly like a light French boulevard comedy except that Ruiz Iriarte is not free to carry the play to its logical and less moral conclusion.[49] Teresa, the title character, was widowed when her daughter was only a year old. As the play opens, it is Marita's wedding day. During the years of her widowhood, Teresa has been a model Spanish mother, totally devoted to her daughter, never going out with men—or so we are led to believe. No sooner has the bride left on her honeymoon than the phone begins to ring and men begin to arrive at the door. One by one, four men arrive, three of them claiming that they love Teresa and that she has told them that once her daughter is married, she will be free to return that love.

The arrival of the various suitors is similar in its comic impact to the arrival of Fernando's guests in *You're Not Dangerous*. The men—Fernando, an architect; Federico, a young architecture student; Nicolás, an Argentinian; and Don José, an older man—immediately view each other as rivals. Teresa herself is somewhat bewildered by their arrival; she has been attracted to so many men in the past several years and, in her double life as an extroverted flirt and traditional Spanish mother, has had so many encounters with men in parks and out-of-the-way places that she seems to have confused them all in her mind. Finally it is learned that Don José is not a suitor at all but has come to buy the apartment and that Teresa is actually married to one of the other three men.

Initially none of the men will admit to being Teresa's husband. The following day, however, all three return and claim to be the man she has secretly married. The matter is only resolved when Marita returns momentarily from her honeymoon and identifies her stepfather, Fernando. She had known all along about her mother's double life and had, in fact, suggested the marriage as a way to keep her mother out of trouble. Fernando, concerned at first that Teresa has deceived him with the other men, is assured of Teresa's fidelity, and all ends happily.

Quite obviously Ruiz Iriarte has built his comedy once again on role playing and role reversal. Teresa, the respectable Spanish woman is, in fact, a flirt. She has merely been playing a role to conform to society's expectation of her. She is, like many of the playwright's heroines, caught between the traditional stereotyped image of what a proper woman is and the emancipated role of women in the postwar period. Although Ruiz Iriarte has not hesitated to portray women of easy virtue in his comedies—Patricia of *When She Is the Other Woman* and Fernando's exmistresses in *You're Not Dangerous*, for example—he generally shies away from showing a wife or even a widow actually taking a lover. His young women, too, are basically virtuous in spite of their sophistication. When Teresa in great embarrassment decides to prepare Marita for her wedding night, Marita merely laughs at her mother. She feels that she is much better equipped to give her mother advice, just as the nieces in *The Rebellious Spinster* and *Child's Play* apparently know more about love and sex than the older women. The roles of the young women and the older women are reversed, but we are not to assume that the younger women have acquired their knowledge through experience. Marita's role, like that of the bride in *The Apprentice Lover*, is also reversed with our expectation in her relationship with the groom. It is he who is nervous and she who takes command of the honeymoon trip.

As a group, Ruiz Iriarte's comedies of manners from the 1950s do not represent his most interesting or important theater. They are, in fact, the plays which give rise to his widespread reputation as a writer of light, escapist comedies based on a single repeated formula. Certainly they are plays with similar plots that show only the middle-class and that avoid major social problems of the period. It is not totally accurate, however, to generalize about the plays. The comedies vary from some (*You're Not Dangerous* and *The Private Life of Mama*) that do resemble French boulevard farces to others (*Child's Play* and *The Poor Little Liar*) that because of their skillful blend of loneliness and anguish within the structure of farce and their portrayal of some well developed characters approach tragicomedy. The repeated figure of the *pobrecito*, in either male or female form, is an important key to Ruiz Iriarte's view of contemporary life. The *pobrecito* is an antihero, misunderstood by a society with an inverted sense of values and hence underrated by individuals within that society. All of the comedies of manners, including those with an undercurrent of tragedy and those with a strong illusion-reality motif as well as the more frivolous ones, are well written farces, guaranteed to entertain an audience. They are also plays which collectively express the playwright's gentle criticism of the customs and moral standards of a changing Spain.

CHAPTER 5

Theater As Fun

FOR Ruiz Iriarte, all theater, whether comic or dramatic, is a "game of the spirit" although he also finds that the definition fits comedy better than any other kind of theater.[1] This concept of "game" or "play," one which underlies many of his own works, is particularly apparent in those farces of poetic fantasy and comedies of manners where the characters within the play see life as a game and, in adopting roles for themselves or in staging elaborate farces for others, create some kind of play within the play. But Ruiz Iriarte also sees the possibility of theater as a "game" on another level, plays that are simply meant as a diversion, in essence a game for the sake of a game. He confesses that for him this dramatic form "as ancient and as fresh, eternal and young as theater itself, holds an irresistible charm and a permanent appeal." He is attracted by a theater that exists solely for the element of play or fun without profound messages or hidden morals. Citing the examples of Shakespeare's *A Midsummer Night's Dream*, as well as certain comedies of Molière, Benavente, and Anouilh, he suggests that this kind of light, diaphanous theater is very difficult to write because it must be done "with the point of the pen, using words like arrows aimed at the sensitivity of the spectator."[2] This latter judgment is one with which a reviewer of one of Ruiz Iriarte's plays concurred when he noticed that there are comedies "of light warp, of intranscendental theme, that require of their author greater effort, greater skill and agility" than plays of more robust themes that seem to grow by themselves.[3]

Some of Ruiz Iriarte's works that we have grouped in other categories, particularly the last two comedies of manners, are light plays, designed primarily to entertain. Nevertheless, because there is some conscious effort on the part of the playwright to reflect aspects of contemporary society, they may not be viewed solely as "theatrical games."[4] There are two of his plays, however, which he has so classified and that do stand apart from his other published works. The first of these, *La guerra empieza en Cuba* [The war begins in Cuba], falls chronologically between *You're Not Dangerous* and *The Private Life of Mama*. The setting is a provincial capital in Spain at the end of the nineteenth century; the farce is based on the classical device of twins. The other, *Un paraguas bajo la lluvia* [An umbrella under the rain], was staged ten years later, immediately following one of the serious dramas, *El carrusell* [The carousel]. Again the play does not deal primarily with the present but rather tells four stories from four different periods of time. Both of the plays were well received and are included in Ruiz Iriarte's personal list of his eight most important successes in the twenty-five year-period up through 1969.[5]

I   The War Begins in Cuba

La guerra empieza en Cuba [The war begins in Cuba] opened in Madrid in November, 1955, and starred Tina Gascó as Adelaida and Juanita. Like Anouilh in his *Invitation to the Chateau* (1947), Ruiz Iriarte has constructed the farce so that the twins, who are the main characters, never appear on stage at the same time; both roles may thus be played by the same actress. In his self-criticism of the play, Ruiz Iriarte mentions that playwrights have used twins as a "pretty toy" to play with from Plautus in Roman comedy through Anouilh and that the device has long tempted him.[6] In spite of the many writers who have used twins as a basis for farce over the centuries, however, Ruiz Iriarte has managed to give to *The War Begins in Cuba* his own original touch. Torrente Ballester has identified two aspects of the farce which possibly are unique to this play: the introduction of a second set of twins and an unexpected change of personality on the part of one of the principal twins that deceives the spectators as well as other characters.[7] At least one critic at the time felt that the play was Ruiz Iriarte's best work.[8] In 1957 it was made into a movie starring Emma Pennella.[9]

In general in his farces and light comedies, Ruiz Iriarte shows himself to be a master craftsman, carefully building his plays on a series of comic situations. This skill is clearly seen in *The War Begins in Cuba* where the scenes follow one another at a rapid pace but with an obvious pattern of linking devices which may be compared to the so-called "well-made play."[10] Each scene flows naturally into the next and the situation or character announced in one appears almost immediately on cue. In addition, a series of reversals in the action helps to maintain the rhythm of the play. Because *The War Begins in Cuba* is written in fun and its greatest strength is its structure, the

most appropriate way to study this farce is by analyzing the development from scene to scene. The play has two acts, the second of which
is divided into two sections.[11] For the purpose of this analysis,
however, we shall define scene divisions by the exits or entrances of
characters that affect the direction of the action. Using such a definition, the first act has thirteen scenes and the two sections of the
second act, twenty and ten respectively. The outline which follows
indicates, beyond necessary exposition, only those aspects of each
scene contributing to overall patterns of anticipation, hence to the
forward movement of the farce.[12]

Act I

Scene 1: The provincial governor's mansion. The Marqués, Pepito and
Margarita are rehearsing an amateur theatrical.

Scene 2: Mariana, Adelaida's mother enters. She mentions that her daughter,
the Governor's wife, is a cold and rigidly moral woman who controls the
province.

Scene 3: Margarita's twin daughters, Rosita and Teresita, enter. They look so
much alike that no one can tell them apart. Their only defect is that they
like to make up stories.

Scene 4: Adelaida enters. She announces that the governor has called off the
amateur theatrical.

Scene 5: The Marqués and Pepito, left alone on the stage, comment that it is
Adelaida, not the Governor, who is in command and that only a daring
libertine without scruples can possibly save the city from Adelaida's au-
thoritarian control.

Scene 6: Enter Javier, a military officer who has been banished to the city as
punishment for being a daring libertine without scruples.

Scene 7: Enter Adelaida. Javier greets her with great familiarity, saying that
they met the night before on the train from Madrid.

Scene 8: Adelaida, left alone with her mother, expresses dismay. Such a
terrible misunderstanding has not happened to her since she and her
mother left Havana twelve years before. The entrance of Teresita and
Rosita reinforces Adelaida's alarm. She mentions that a ship of repatriates
has reached Spain from Cuba.

Scene 9: Enter the maid. She is amazed to see Adelaida there because she has
just seen her strolling on the sidewalk in front of the house. Exit Adelaida.

Scene 10: Mariana confesses to the maid that the woman on the sidewalk is
Adelaida's twin sister Juanita. Completely opposite in character from her
sister, Juanita had dishonored the family by running away with an engineer. Because of the scandal, Mariana had brought Adelaida to Spain to
find her a suitable husband. She pledges the maid to secrecy.

Scene 11: Enter Juanita. She accuses her mother, who had always favored

Adelaida, and her sister of having caused her own unhappy life. She vows
vengeance and implies that she will pretend to be her sister.
Scene 12: Juanita is left alone. Enter Javier. They kiss and agree to meet that
night at a hotel. They are seen and overheard by Rosita and Teresita.
Scene 13: Mariana returns, finding only the twins who say they have seen
nothing.

A review of the first act indicates that Ruiz Iriarte has skillfully
presented the basic elements of his plot. Before Adelaida appears on
stage, we are already prepared for her stern, unloving personality.
We are not surprised that she cancels the play or that others would
delight in seeing her downfall. The introduction of the twins Teresita
and Rosita prepares us not only for the discovery that Adelaida has a
twin sister but also allows us to anticipate some mischief on the part of
the story telling sisters after they see Javier and the woman they
presume to be the Governor's wife together. The stage is set for a
classic case of mistaken identity in which people will believe that the
actions of the fun-loving Juanita are those of her stern look-alike.

Act II. Section I.
Scenes 1-2: The next morning. Mariana and Adelaida receive a visit from
Pepa, Juanita's friend and companion. She announces that Juanita only
asks to play the role of the Governor's wife for a day.
Scene 3: Adelaida says that she knows what Juanita is planning and that she
will outsmart her. She and Mariana exit.
Scenes 4-5: Enter the Governor. He complains to his secretary that his wife
treats him like a *pobrecito* and shows him no affection. He is overheard by a
woman who seems to be Juanita.
Scenes 6-9: Enter "Juanita." She stuns the Governor by treating him with
affection. Mariana is appalled.
Scenes 10-13: Arrivals of Margarita, Teresita, Rosita, the Marqués and
Pepito, all of whom think that the Governor's wife has spent the night at the
hotel with Javier. Javier also arrives and, believing that they already know
about Juanita, talks of his new love. Comic misunderstanding.
Scene 14: Enter a smiling Adelaida who announces that the play will be given
after all. She and Javier apparently do not know each other. Exit Adelaida.
Scene 15: Javier denies having spent the night with the Governor's wife.
Scenes 16-17: Margarita accuses her daughters of making up stories again.
Reversal for the twins.
Scenes 18-19: Juanita and Pepa arrive. Mariana realizes that Adelaida has
deliberately assumed the personality of her sister (Scenes 6-9, Scene 14).
Scene 20: Enter Javier. He asks Mariana for permission to marry Juanita.

In this first section of the second act, Ruiz Iriarte has continued to build on the situation of mistaken identity which we anticipated at the end of the first act. Several characters, who do not know that Adelaida has a twin sister, have attributed Juanita's actions to Adelaida. The misunderstanding is further developed in the initial conversations with Javier, who because he thinks that they know there are two sisters therefore makes statements which have a scandalous meaning for his listeners, who erroneously believe they apply to the Governor's wife. Parallel with this case of wrong identity is an additional confusion on the part of Mariana, the maid, and the audience, who have mistaken Adelaida for Juanita. This second misunderstanding is clarified by the end of the section. But the rest of the characters still are not in on the secret and the twins are discredited. As the section ends, we anticipate that the sisters will attempt to clarify the mystery in order to achieve a second reversal in their own situation.

Act II. Section II.
Scenes 1-3: Teresita and Rosita plot to prove that their story about seeing Javier kiss someone who looked like the Governor's wife was true. They reenact the scene with an unsuspecting Pepito, switching Rosita for Teresita.
Scenes 4-5: Margarita and the Marqués witness the kiss. With their resultant explanation, the twins convince the others that Adelaida has a look-alike. Second reversal. They exit.
Scenes 6-8: Juanita and Javier declare their love for each other and go off together.
Scene 9: A transformed Adelaida returns in triumph from giving a speech at a dedication ceremony. She tells her mother that in the future she will be a warm and loving person like Juanita.
Scene 10: Enter Rosita, Teresita, the Marqués, Pepito and Margarita. The twins identify Adelaida as "the other woman." The Marqués says something insulting about the Governor's wife, only to discover that he is talking to the real Adelaida. The play ends with Margarita once again convinced that her daughters made the story up and should be punished. Third reversal for the twins.

In the final section of the play, Ruiz Iriarte presents the anticipated explanation of Teresita and Rosita by introducing a play within the play that represents another example of mistaken identity. We know that the twins' theory is correct, but the departure of Juanita eliminates the possibility that the others will ever see the two sisters together. In the final scene, Ruiz Iriarte reverses the mistaken identity of the first act, having the twins now mistake Adelaida for Juanita as they had earlier mistaken Juanita for Adelaida. The sisters, who have deliberately confused others for fun in the past, are now themselves victims of the same kind of confusion—but with no opportunity to prove their innocence. The farce thus ends on a note of comic irony.

II   An umbrella under the rain

While the primary source of humor in *The War Begins in Cuba* is in the clever manipulation of mistaken identities, the farce also exploits the comic contrasts of its historical setting. Costumes and customs from other periods can be funny to us, and writers of comedies frequently use them as laugh-producing devices. Such is the case in *Un paraguas bajo la lluvia* [An umbrella under the rain], in which Ruiz Iriarte presents scenes from 1885, 1905, 1936, and the present. The play, which opened in Madrid in September, 1965, was directed by the playwright.

As the play begins, the stage is in darkness except for a feeble light directed on a platform at the front. A disconsolate Florita, sitting there under an umbrella, is calling for her dead mother. In answer to her prayers, Doña Florita appears. She had died when her daughter was a child and part of the humor in the ensuing scene, aside from the comic potential in the ghost figure itself, stems from her surprise at the changes that have occurred since her death.[13] Florita confides to her mother that she has love problems. Her mother responds that all of the Floritas, from this Florita's great-grandmother on, have had the same trouble. She thus introduces the first in a series of four stories, which are enacted on the main part of the stage. Following each scene, the action returns to the platform where Florita and the ghost continue their conversation. The transition between the two stage locations is accomplished by appropriate use of spotlights, while the differing time periods are indicated by slight changes in the stage setting and background music from the various periods.

The story that unfolds around the original Florita is basically the same love triangle which will recur in the other three generations as well. Florita is always a young woman of rather unassuming appearance who must compete for the man she loves against a much more physically attractive rival. It is by using her wits that Florita achieves her goal. In each case the three roles are played by the same actor and actresses. The structure of the play has prompted one critic to use musical nomenclature and call it "variations on a theme."[14]

The first Florita is a maid and excellent cook who decides to pursue Octavio, a marquis who has spent two weeks vacation with the people

for whom she works and has obviously relished the food she prepared. When she arrives at his bachelor apartment, he is entertaining
the beautiful Adelina, a woman of easy virtue who has picked Octavio
to be the next in her series of lovers. Throughout most of the scene a
nervous Octavio attempts to keep the two women from discovering
each other, particularly as he has told Adelina that he has no maid and
Adelina keeps reappearing from his bedroom wearing less and less
clothing. Florita finally confronts Adelina and has Octavio throw her
out, thus proving that the way to Octavio's heart is through his
stomach.

In the next story, Rosalía, the wife of the marquis' first cousin, is
having an affair with Teodoro, a young man with whom the second
Florita is in love. The basic farcical situation of the scene is a stock one
in which the younger Rosalía hopes to prevent her old husband from
learning about her lover. Florita knows the truth, however, and
eventually turns the situation to her own advantage. She tells Rosalía's husband that Teodoro visits the apartment every day while he is
gone but that the purpose of his visits is to court Florita. Don Leandro
believes the story and promises that the two sweethearts will be
married within a month. Florita gives Teodoro a chance to run away
from the trap that she has set for him, but because her confession of
love touches him, he remains.

The third story, that of Doña Florita herself, takes place in Madrid
on July 18, 1936. Florita, already a confirmed spinster, is having a
birthday party. Her guests Adolfo and Guillermina become engaged
and break the happy news to Florita. Florita, who has loved Adolfo
since they were children, tries to prevent the marriage by telling each
of them a lie about the other. Guillermina departs in anger just before
the sound of shots in the streets announces the outbreak of the
Spanish Civil War. Florita convinces Adolfo that it would be very
dangerous for him to leave because he is a known conservative. With
this excuse, she keeps him locked up in her apartment for the three
years of the war.

In one of Jardiel Poncela's last plays, *El sexo débil ha hecho
gimnasia* [The weaker sex has undergone gymnastics, 1946], he, too,
contrasted women of the nineteenth century with those of the twentieth, showing the latter to be much more aggressive and emancipated. Ruiz Iriarte's conclusion is similar. The Florita of each
succeeding generation is more dominant and more deceitful than her
mother. The obvious extension of this pattern is the situation in the
fourth story in which the roles of the two sexes are diametrically

opposed to traditional ones. Florita has driven Mateo to a tourist inn seventy kilometers from Madrid. Because of a heavy rainstorm, they are forced to spend the night there and she plans to take advantage of him. Florita's rival this time is a provocative movie starlet who is also stranded at the inn. The catalyst for Florita's rape of Mateo, however, is Nina's innuendo that Mateo is a homosexual. When Mateo finally explains to Florita that he had resisted her advances because he was a virgin, not because he did not love her, she agrees to make an honest man of him by marrying him.

Ruiz Iriarte himself has said that *An Umbrella Under the Rain* is based on a warm and tender immorality; [15] and indeed, there is a certain amount of risqué humor in the play. The sexual themes are more overt in this farce than in the other works analyzed thus far in the present study. The change may be attributed to a slight relaxation in censorship after 1963 which allowed more freedom of expression in the Spanish theater on such matters than in the preceding two decades. [16] Beyond the sexual references, the humor of *An Umbrella Under the Rain* is based on stock situations and devices, notably the use of the ghost, the contrast among several periods of time, and the shifting roles of the two sexes. The work does not pretend to hold any profound meaning but does prove the playwright's contention that theater can be fun.

CHAPTER 6

The Serious Dramas

THE noted Spanish theater critic Alfredo Marqueríe classified Ruiz Iriarte twenty years ago as a writer of comedies who might have been a serious dramatist.[1] His comment, which has become the most frequently quoted single observation about the Spanish playwright, from the perspective of the present is no longer completely accurate. Ruiz Iriarte who himself sees comedy as the most important component of his writing career, states that he loves the genre and considers it the synthesis of all kinds of theater from vaudeville and farce to drama and tragedy.[2] Nevertheless he has written serious dramas, particularly in the decade of the 1960s, and these works rank among his best plays. Holt is quite correct when he points out that the great popularity associated with Ruiz Iriarte's lighter comedies should not obscure the value of his excellent mature dramas.[3]

Clearly the culmination of Ruiz Iriarte's efforts as a serious dramatist may be found in three of his later works: *El carrusell* [The carousel], *La señora recibe una carta* [The lady receives a letter], and *Historia de un adulterio* [Story of adultery]. The playwright includes *The Carousel* and *Story of Adultery* as two of his eight most important successes.[4] Lendínez-Gallego is wrong, however, when he states that "the year 1964 and his work *The Carousel* mark a surprising change" in the playwright's orientation.[5] As Schevill notes, Ruiz Iriarte revealed his talent as a writer of drama in the unpublished play *Los pájaros ciegos* [Blind birds, 1948], in the "short but almost painfully tragic dialogue" *Juanita va a Rio de Janeiro* [Juanita goes to Rio de Janeiro, 1948], and in *Esta noche es la víspera* [Tonight is the prelude, 1958].[6] Moreover, as we have already seen, there is a serious and even tragic undercurrent in many of the lighter comedies. The dramas tend to view the same human problems and flaws in contemporary society that Ruiz Iriarte deals with in his comedies and farces, only now shown in a different light. *Juanita goes to Rio de Janeiro* and *Tonight Is the Prelude* reveal once again conflict in amorous relationships.[7] The three later plays are in some respects an extension of the

comedies of manners, for Ruiz Iriarte develops in depth the loss of
values and the disintegration of the family he sees occurring in an
overly materialistic age. It is in this vein that Molero Manglano
declares *The Carousel* to be a synthesis of all the comedies that
preceded it and then compares the later drama specifically with
Child's Play.[8] With his dramas Ruiz Iriarte not only established
conclusively that the writer of light comedies may be making a serious
commentary on human nature and society's attitudes but also proves
that he, himself, is a multifaceted playwright.

I   Juanita Goes to Rio de Janeiro

In the years following the Civil War, there have been a number of
small "chamber" theaters active in Spain. In general these have been
private groups formed for the purpose of presenting experimental
works not acceptable on the commercial stage. It was for a chamber
theater, directed by José Luis Alfonso, that Ruiz Iriarte wrote his
one-act dramatic dialogue *Juanita va a Rio de Janeiro* [Juanita goes to
Rio de Janeiro]. In his early comedies Ruiz Iriarte frequently introduces male characters who seduce or plan to seduce innocent young
women. The theme appears in *Academy of Love, The Six-Horse
Landau, Child's Play*, and *The Flowers Cafe*. In these plays, which
were produced on the commercial stage, he does not actually show
the seduction scene nor does he dwell in detail on the impact the
man's action may have on the life of the woman. In each case,
however, it is fairly clear that the woman has been in love with the
man while he has viewed her merely as a means of gratifying his
desires or bolstering his ego. It is this underlying conflict between the
two sexes which forms the basis for *Juanita Goes to Rio de Janeiro*.

Juanita has been a virtuous young woman, filled with illusions
about love and life. Rio de Janeiro is the symbol she uses for her
dreams; when she is with Jorge in fact, she feels that her dream has
been realized and that she has "gone to Rio." The scene of the brief
play is a house of ill repute where Jorge has brought her for the
purpose of seducing her. He is appalled that she is happy afterwards,
not remorseful. His cold attitude destroys her happiness and makes
her realize that Jorge has brought a series of young women to this
same house. Because he does not love her at all but has merely used
her, her illusions are shattered and she feels that she is no longer
pure. Her final lines are, "I shall never be again what I was. After
today I shall be bad . . . very bad." [9] The little play is very short,

without time for any real development of character. Ruiz Iriarte's principal purpose seems to be to underscore the tragic implications of seduction and to criticize a certain kind of male attitude toward women.

II Tonight Is the Prelude

Esta noche es la víspera [Tonight is the prelude] opened in Madrid in December, 1958, but its conception actually dates from 1955. Ruiz Iriarte has explained that he began work on the play at the same time he started *The War Begins in Cuba* but, finding the structure difficult to develop, set it aside for several years.[10] Schevill and Holt both consider *Tonight Is the Prelude* to be serious drama and Judith S. Merrill in the introduction to her student edition of the play calls it one of Ruiz Iriarte's "best and most serious" plays.[11] While these observations are not unfounded, in some respects the play, which resembles high comedy rather than serious drama, may be viewed as a transitional work linking the light comedies of the 1950s to the more serious theater of the 1960s. As one critic noted at the time of the première, *Tonight Is the Prelude* "represents the abandonment of one style and the attempt to travel another road but using the old experience in order not to stumble."[12]

The play consists of two acts preceded by a prologue. As the prologue begins, Elvira, an elegant young woman, and Daniel, a man in his thirties who walks with some difficulty and uses a cane, enter the living room of a country home. They had been passing by the house on their way to France when Elvira became attracted by the"For Sale" sign. As the scene progresses it becomes apparent, however, that the house is somehow familiar to Elvira. When Daniel asks her if she ever considered leaving him during the recent illness that might have left him permanently crippled, she responds by telling him a story. Her story is the play itself, which is thus established as a long flashback. Holt observes that Ruiz Iriarte will use related flashback techniques more imaginatively in several of his later plays.[13]

The action of the prologue takes place in summer. The time of the first act is the previous winter. It is a snowy night and a small commercial airplane has been forced to land in a field near this same deserted country home not far from the Pyrenees. The accident affects twelve passengers who thus find themselves brought together by chance. During a long night's vigil while the pilot goes for help, they gradually begin to reveal to one another their true identities and their problems. Their confessions are precipitated not only by the circumstances themselves but also by a device sometimes used in mystery plays. One of the passengers, Don Joaquín, tells another, Valentín, that someone in the group is a policeman in disguise. This prompts Valentín to inform the others that one of them is "guilty," that is to say, that one of them is going to Paris to commit a crime. The suspicions and fears aroused by this comment lead several of the characters to question one another more intensively than they might otherwise do. The presence in the group of a young working-class priest also tends to make them question themselves as to their real motives in making the trip. The explanation of the title and the theme of the play are expressed by Valentín in the first act where he defends the rights of the alleged criminal in their midst: "Tonight is the prelude, and no one has the right to restrain his freedom. Who is a sinner on the eve of the sin? No one. Because the sin does not yet exist . . . He can still choose. That's the terrible part. Life is an eternal, anguished eve. One can always choose, always." [14] By the end of the play, six of the characters, including Valentín, determine that their reasons for going to Paris are wrong and elect to return to Madrid instead.

Ruiz Iriarte acknowledged that *Tonight Is the Prelude* was not a theater of his own invention. [15] Other critics, of course, have also noted the existence of many plays in which various characters are thrown together in an isolated place because of an accident or other circumstance. [16] To cite only one example of many possible ones, there is the precedent of John Steinbeck's *The Wayward Bus* (1947). Anouilh, the playwright judged by Ruiz Iriarte to be the best in the contemporary theater, has one of his characters state in his recent play *Cher Antoine ou l'amour raté* [Dear Antoine or The love that failed, 1969-70]: "I hope you notice that this is getting more like one of Antoine's plays. People come here, there and everywhere, on some chance pretext, with no desire to meet, yet flung together by some outside agency, somewhere. It's a very old theatrical device and he adored it. He used it again and again." [17]

Tonight Is the Prelude, however, relates not only to this kind of theater but to other current devices as well. The flashback technique and even the atmosphere created in the prologue when Elvira seems mystified by the familiarity of her surroundings may reflect the influence of J. B. Priestley. Marqueríe suggests parallels with *Dangerous Corner* (1932) and *I Have Been Here Before* (1938). [18] Priestley's plays enjoyed great popularity in Madrid in the 1950s; Sainz de Robles reports productions of the British playwright's works in his yearbooks for 1949-50, 1950-51, 1955-56, 1959-60. The interest in Priestley related to a vogue of mystery plays in general, a subgenre to which *Tonight Is the Prelude* also partially belongs. This is the period when Mihura and Paso wrote a number of detective stories or parodies of detective stories.[19] Ruiz Iriarte also tried his hand at them in his unpublished *Una investigación privada* [A private investigation, 1959].[20] An unquestionable influence on the Spanish subgenre was Agatha Christie, five of whose plays were staged in Madrid between 1954-55 and 1959-60 according to Sainz de Robles. The first of these, *The Mousetrap*, opened in Madrid on November 12, 1954, shortly before Ruiz Iriarte began work on *Tonight Is the Prelude*. In common with Ruiz Iriarte's play, the Christie mystery takes place in an isolated home in the country where the characters are cut off from the outside world by a snowstorm. The telephone ceases to function. They learn that in their midst is a policeman, ultimately to discover that it is the wrong person they so identify. They also know that there is a murderer in the group and hence begin to ask each other questions and to suspect one another. All of these aspects are repeated with some modification in the later Spanish play.

In spite of the obvious borrowing of current and traditional devices, *Tonight Is the Prelude* bears the unique stamp of its author. One critic in his review in fact decided not to mention how much "Ruiz Iriarte resembles Ruiz Iriarte" in the play.[21] The resemblance occurs in the comic tone of some of the dialogue, in the introduction of certain characters he has used before including the *pobrecito*, and in the underlying faith in humanity which manifests itself in the morally correct decisions taken by the six people who elect to return to Madrid. In terms of a specific parallel, the earlier work with which *Tonight Is the Prelude* probably has the most in common is *The Flowers Cafe*. Both plays bring together a group of characters of varying social and economic backgrounds who share a common personal problem or moral dilemma. And in both cases a person who was planning to leave his or her spouse has second thoughts as the result of an accident that delays his or her departure. In *The Flowers Cafe*, Gonzalo's car broke down preventing his desertion; in *Tonight Is the Prelude*, the emergency landing gives Elvira an extra evening in which to analyze her own actions.

Ruiz Iriarte's major concern with *Tonight Is the Prelude* and his reason for delaying its completion was the structural difficulty pre-

sented by its one stage setting and two uninterrupted hours of action.[22] The intermission does not really represent a break because the
second act continues at the moment when the first act ends. The
playwright has solved his problem with a variety of techniques.
Initially he prevents the scene from becoming static through the use
of comic characters and situations. Don Joaquín is a *pobrecito*; every
time he attempts to make friends with someone or start up a conversation, he is shunted aside and ignored. Anita, a middle-aged widow, is
very conservative and very proud of it. Rosa, on the other hand, is
obviously a woman of doubtful background. Conflict between the two
is inevitable. Avelina and Javier are newlyweds; their situation leads
to some suggestive comments concerning their wedding night. In
addition to these comic touches, Ruiz Iriarte introduces the "mystery" of the policeman and the alleged criminal during the first act,
thus creating a certain amount of tension and expectation. As the
grounded passengers begin to pose each other questions, it becomes
apparent that Elvira is hiding something. Anita is sure that Elvira was
not traveling alone even though she now says she is. At the close of
the first act we learn that Elvira is actually with the novelist Marcos;
she is abandoning her sick husband and running away with her lover.
The second act thus begins with our anticipation that the others will
learn of this clandestine relationship. Although the Elvira-Marcos
story is central to the action, other characters have secrets as well,
thus adding to the level of expectation.

Marcos, in the middle of the first act when the various characters
begin introducing themselves to each other, suggests that Paris is
where people who are running away go. "We are all fleeing from
something. Or going in search of something, which is a way of fleeing
from everything else" (*N*, 232). As it turns out, he is right with respect
at least to several of the characters. Elvira is fleeing from the responsibility and burden of a crippled husband in an attempt to find happiness and love. Anita is fleeing from time, hoping to have a last fling
with a man who awaits her in Paris. Rosa, who has been Javier's
mistress and had financed his education, is fleeing from his betrayal
and seeking to destroy his marriage. Valentín is going to Paris in order
to join in an illegal scheme which will allow him to escape from
poverty. Another young man in the group, also of the lower economic
class, is going to Paris to join a wealthy male lover.[23] A young woman,
who initially pretends not to understand Spanish, is running away
from home because her widowed father has just remarried. At the
end, perhaps moved by the words of the priest, these six choose to

reverse their paths and let the others go on without them. There are many kinds of crime, the priest tells them, not just the obvious ones that relate to the law and the police, but others as well. "They are the secret crimes that hate, desire, ambition, pride, vengeance are capable of committing. And we are all guilty of those crimes. Man is an eternal fugitive, pursued by his little and big crimes. Because crime is everywhere; it is hidden in everything; even in the most noble appearances. It is behind that which is most pure. Even at the bottom of love itself. . ." (*N*, 275).

The most frequent criticism leveled at Ruiz Iriarte's play is that the ending is too idealistic, almost miraculous. "Although *Tonight Is the Prelude* deals convincingly with the questions of conscience and free will, the author's estimate of human capacities for self-redemption may seem overly optimistic in a particularly cynical age."[24] In spite of this defect, the play has been highly praised by many, perhaps because it was perceived as being a more serious, more philosophical work than Ruiz Iriarte's lighter comedies. In this vein, one critic who called it Ruiz Iriarte's best work to date remarked that it was "the most complete, the most effective, and the one of most consequence."[25]

III   The Carousel

El carrusell [The carousel] opened in Madrid in December, 1964, following a four-year period in which Ruiz Iriarte had staged no new original plays. The production starred Enrique Diosdado and Amelia de la Torre, the actors who are associated with four of the playwright's important works of the decade. One of Ruiz Iriarte's most successful plays, *The Carousel* premièred in Barcelona in March, 1965, and was seen in forty-five other cities of northern Spain that summer when the Diosdado company went on tour.[26] It is one of Ruiz Iriarte's favorite plays and one that clearly reflects his observations of contemporary Spanish society, particularly of a certain "shining, frivolous, carefree" sector of that society.[27]

The Carousel is the work immediately preceding *An Umbrella Under the Rain*; from a structural point of view, the two plays have much in common. In the latter farce, the central character calls forth the ghost of her mother. Their ensuing conversation is interrupted at intervals by long sequences from the past. Similarly in *The Carousel* the central figure, Daniel de Sandoval, has evoked a supernatural character, in this case a godlike police commissioner, to whom he confesses a story from the past. The first act of the play is divided into five scenes and the second act into two. The conversations between Daniel and the commissioner take place in the first, third, and seventh scenes, all of which are short. The transitions between the dialogue with the supernatural figure and the flashbacks are handled, as in *An Umbrella Under the Rain*, by use of special lighting and musical effects. The staging technique is not unlike the development of two planes of reality employed by Arthur Miller in *Death of a Salesman* (1949), a play widely acclaimed in Spain. The compassionate figure of the police commissioner and the flashbacks may also be somewhat related to another Miller play, *A View From the Bridge* (1955).

The tone of the first scene is serious. Daniel indicates to the police commissioner that he is looking for a guilty person. The mood swiftly changes in the second scene, however, to one of farce. Daniel and his wife are caricatures; their comments and actions are exaggerated. Rita is frivolous, talkative, and hypocritical. Daniel is a man immersed in his business. They are the stereotype of a materialistic, social-climbing upper middle-class couple. In the third scene, Daniel makes just this kind of commentary to the commissioner. "Everyone has a game," he says. "We are all very frivolous. . . . But can we be any other way?" [28] They are a product of their society. Moreover as a business man, he has had to fight, to destroy others or be himself destroyed. If such a man fails, the result is grotesque. But if he wins, it is tragic. In either case, life is a spectacle (*CA*, 307).

These first three scenes are all short and serve primarily as an introduction to the fourth scene in which we meet the four children of Daniel and Rita. Though Maribel, Ramonín, Tomy and Lolín are very different from each other in their personalities and interests, all feel alienated from their superficial parents. Initially the scene is again comic, with lighthearted banter occurring among the young people. But the tone changes when Lolín, the youngest, begins to cry. She feels very much alone in life. Lolín's complaints about their parents and about the lack of communication even among the brothers and sisters provides the opening for Maribel to reveal that she has fallen in love and plans to marry an engineer from Guinea within a month. Her story of how she met her fiancé is again farcical in tone, but other subtextual hints in the action have suggested the possibility that the brothers, particularly the bohemian Ramonín, have their own secret problems. By the end of the scene, we learn that Ramonín's friend Michel is wanted by the police and we know that Tomy, the studious brother, is in love with Mónica, the family's attractive young maid.

The beginning of the fifth scene stands in sharp contrast to the mood at the end of the preceding one. Daniel and Rita return from another in their endless series of parties. Their chatter is superficial, as always. Maribel attempts to tell her parents that she is in love, but they are too preoccupied with themselves to listen to her. At Lolín's suggestion, the four young people decide to invent a game in order to punish their parents. Each one of them will pretend to have a serious problem, thereby shocking their parents out of their egotism. Accordingly Tomy tells his parents that he is going to become a father. They are horrified, but so is Mónica, who has been trying unsuccessfully all evening to tell Tomy that she really is pregnant. The "games" of the children follow in rapid order. Lolín says that she has pneumonia. Maribel walks out of the house, slamming the door behind her, and Lolín announces that her sister has run off to Guinea. Ramonín calls home and says that he is in jail. The series of disasters is too much for Rita, who faints. Taking pity on her mother, Lolín confesses that the stories are all lies.

The second act takes place the following morning. Ramonín, who has been out all night, returns home and reveals to Tomy that he really was in jail when he called the previous evening. He was released only after Michel confessed his sole responsibility for an unidentified crime. Ramonín swears Tomy to secrecy. Mónica subsequently tells Tomy that everyone—the servants, the people in the neighborhood, everyone except the family—knew about Ramonín and Michel (*CA*, 368). The implication here, as Holt has noted, is that Michel and Ramonín have had a homosexual relationship.[29] Tomy, who really loves Mónica and is happy about the baby, assures her that they will be married. Not knowing that Lolín has confessed that the four problems were lies, he goes to talk to his parents. They, in turn, decide to play their own game.

Initially, before Lolín tells the others that she had confessed the plot to their parents the night before, Rita and Daniel pretend to believe the stories they assume to be false. Gradually they realize that all the stories except Lolín's pneumonia are based on truth, but they refuse to acknowledge that the sons' problems are real. When Maribel returns home and tells her mother about her fiancé, Rita enthusiastically begins planning a big wedding; but she and Daniel deliberately reject the truth about either Ramonín or Tomy. Mónica overhears them say that they will send Tomy away. Unconcerned about the plight of their little maid, Daniel and Rita set off on another day of endless business and social activities.

In the final scene Daniel reveals to the commissioner that the dejected Mónica threw herself in front of a bus. "Who killed Mónica?" he asks. "The game," replies the commissioner. "No one is guilty, but there is always a victim" (*CA*, 392). Life, he adds later, is a carousel: "The carousel is always in motion. Night and day. It is like an enchanted world. A marvelous paradise. But, suddenly, one day the beautiful fair is interrupted, no one knows why. The great carousel stops. The lights go out. It becomes infinite night. An immense shadow envelops everything in the darkness. And then there is always a man who is afraid and who shouts, calling with all his might for a policeman in the midst of the darkness" (*CA*, 394). But afterwards, when the commissioner has come and heard the story, the carousel merely goes on. As the play ends, Rita proves the commissioner's point by entering and speaking to Daniel in her usual frivolous tone. The commissioner, in the meantime, has disappeared.

In *The Carousel* Ruiz Iriarte views with sadness a certain stratum of society. Repeating a theme he had earlier developed in some of the comedies of manners, he shows how the overemphasis on material things and on the social whirl has eroded both traditional values and the family structure itself. He does so without overt moralizing and without attributing responsibility to any individual. In a subtle way, however, he reiterates the thought, also implicit in *Tonight Is the Prelude*, that degeneration of society is related to the loss of religious faith. The godlike commissioner here, like the working-class priest in the earlier play, conveys the message that the game of life may lead us to commit spiritual crimes against others. Significantly Daniel asks if frivolity dominates when faith is gone (*CA*, 385). Tomy later suggests that Ramonín is anguished and alone because he no longer believes in God (*CA*, 385).

Holt is quite correct in observing that *The Carousel* represents "a synthesis of the playwright's major dramatic concerns and techniques."[30] Both the metaphor of the title and the vision of human foibles do, for example, remind one of *The Grand Minuet*. But the most obvious parallel, as both Holt and Molero Manglano have pointed out, is with *Child's Play*.[31] In both cases the children invent a game in order to shock adults into mending their ways and in both cases the game proves to be dangerous as the line between truth and fiction disappears.

The levels of illusion and reality in *The Carousel* are more complex than in *Child's Play* and may more appropriately be labeled Pirandellian.[32] The characters develop games within games as they convert both fiction to truth and truth to fiction, always in the hope of creating a reality more acceptable to them. Truth becomes so relative at some points in the play that the audience, too, begins to wonder what is real and what is not. Was Ramonín really in jail? Where did Maribel spend the night? Do Rita and Daniel realize that Mónica is really pregnant? Ultimately we learn the answers to the questions, but the ambiguity is at least temporarily maintained. Daniel apparently knows that Ramonín was in jail but prefers to accept Lolín's explanation that all of the little dramas were lies. Happier with the fiction, he chooses not to seek the truth. Ramonín has told Tomy that it is better to believe, as Lolín genuinely does, that nothing has happened. "Didn't you see with what happiness Mama discovered that it was all a farce? Didn't you see how simply Papa grasped at the idea that everything was a lie?" (*CA*, 383). It is better, he concludes, to forget and to remain silent than to unleash the truth. In the game they elect to play, appearances are more important than reality.

The Carousel has been compared with Priestley's *An Inspector Calls* (1945).[33] In the British play a mysterious police inspector arrives at the home of a wealthy industrialist. In the interrogation which follows, he eventually proves that all of the members of the family share responsibility in the suicide of a desperate young woman who, like Ruiz Iriarte's Mónica, was carrying the child of one of the sons in the family. Both plays reveal the lack of real communication and understanding between parents and children and the hypocrisy of a middle-class society that voluntarily blinds itself to its own shortcomings. Again, in both cases, the family as a whole attempts to reject the truth of the sordid story while one or two of the family members are not willing or able to forget their own responsibility and guilt. Ruiz Iriarte's play differs from Priestley's in several ways, however. The flashback technique is not present in the British work. The deliberate games and varying levels of truth and fiction are likewise absent from *An Inspector Calls*. Priestley does probe for the truth beneath the socially acceptable façade of his characters, but his technique is not related to the Pirandellian mode as is Ruiz Iriarte's. Moreover the tone of *An Inspector Calls* is that of serious drama throughout while the Spanish playwright continues to juxtapose farce and pathos in order to achieve an effect perhaps closer to tragicomedy.

In some ways *The Carousel* is also related to the *pièces grinçantes* (jarring plays) of Anouilh. As has been mentioned earlier, Anouilh, too, reflects the influence of Pirandello. His plays often depict characters who deliberately assume roles. There are varying levels of reality, and Anouilh may achieve "the revelation of the true by way of the false." [34] The French playwright, like Ruiz Iriarte, observes and criticizes the society around him. He uses "bourgeois family scenes to express his contempt and scorn for the vulgar and hypocritical middle class." [35] Anouilh's theater is usually a blend of the comic and the serious, as is Ruiz Iriarte's; it is in this sense that the parallelism is most striking. As an example of a "jarring play," one may examine *Ardèle ou la Marguerite* (1948), a work called a "vaudeville farce with tragic consequences" by Alba della Fazia.[36] As is true in *The Carousel*, characters are presented as caricatures, exaggerated stereotypes of the hypocritical upper middle-class. Ruiz Iriarte's Daniel is an adulterer—even Lolín knows about her father—but he and Rita are appalled at what people will say if Tomy fathers an illegitimate child or marries beneath his social class. Anouilh's General openly maintains a mistress, but he and the family are distressed at what others will say if his hunchbacked sister Ardèle marries. At the end Ardèle and the man she loves commit suicide and the children in the family are left to wonder at the example their parents set. Anouilh is undoubtedly more cruel in his satire than Ruiz Iriarte, but both playwrights achieve a serious criticism of society through the use of farce.

In *The Carousel* Ruiz Iriarte makes clear his intention of satirizing the foibles of humanity in general and of postwar Spanish society in particular. If his previous "escapist" comedies subtly revealed the attitudes of his audience through their avoidance of painful reality, in *The Carousel* that same message is made explicit. Rita, and, to a lesser extent, Daniel, do not want to know the truth. A problem that is not directly stated does not for them exist. Ramonín will outgrow his difficulties, including his possible homosexuality. Tomy can be sent away. Mónica and the baby will somehow disappear. The play is an indirect commentary on the rationale for censorship itself. Under cover of silence, problems can simply be ignored. Throughout his career Ruiz Iriarte has written about and for the Spanish middle-class. His subject matter and his audience have not changed in *The Carousel*, but here he has set aside his rose-colored glasses and presents his vision of that society in a harsher, more critical light.

IV   The Lady Receives a Letter

In *La señora recibe una carta* [The lady receives a letter] Ruiz

Iriarte continues to focus his attention on a frivolous sector of high society; but his critical tone is muted and the social commentary is rather limited. The play which opened in Madrid in the fall of 1967, like the other works we have grouped under serious drama, is called a comedy by its author.[37] It is, however, more consistently serious in tone than either *Tonight Is the Prelude* or *The Carousel*. The action centers in the elegant apartment of Alberto, a playwright, and his wife Adela. They have invited several friends in for the evening: Tomás, a motion picture director, and his wife Alicia; Manuel, a stockbroker, and his wife Teresa; Laura, a famous movie actress; and Marina, Alberto's young secretary. The atmosphere is relaxed and pleasant, although there are indications of tensions between some of the characters. Adela suffers pangs of jealousy. Tomás and Alicia are extravagant people who spend more than he earns. Laura, now a mature woman, resents the happiness of the married couples. Manuel, as a respectable businessman, stands almost as a comic foil to his frivolous, artistic friends.

Somewhat bored, the group seeks diversion. Adela suggests playing the "game of truth" in which each of them will honestly reveal their opinions of the others. This idea is rejected in favor of Alberto's reading them his latest play. He reaches the point in his script where a mysterious stranger arrives at the door. At that moment his own doorbell rings and Adela finds that an anonymous note has been left for the lady of the house. The note alleges that among her guests is her husband's mistress. Adela and the others all believe the note to be true and begin to interrogate and accuse one another in order to identify Alberto's mistress. Alberto protests his innocence in vain. By the end of the first act, he learns that the note was left outside his door by mistake, but in order to avenge himself for their lack of faith in him, chooses not to reveal this to the others.

In the second act, before the others, too, learn that the note was meant for the people next door, the four women and two men continue their search for the guilty person. In the course of their investigation, they discover a number of secrets from the past. Laura had had a short affair with Alberto before his marriage. Alicia had known Alberto before she met and married Tomás. Teresa had loved Alberto and had lost him to Adela. But it is Marina for whom the inadvertent "game of truth" has the most impact. She really is in love with Alberto and, although there has never been an affair between her and Alberto, he has employed her as a secretary in order to gratify his ego. As the play ends, Adela destroys the anonymous note so that it cannot harm others as it already has her and her friends. Marina, who leaves the apartment in a state of anguish and despair, has nevertheless been saved from potential exploitation by the "little miracle" of the anonymous letter. The others decide they need one another too much to let the confessions of one evening destroy the friendship of many years.

The Lady Receives a Letter bears a number of similarities to other works by Ruiz Iriarte. The potential love triangle involving Adela, Alberto and Alberto's secretary is not unlike that of Child's Play, and the other men suggest that Alberto, too, is something of a Don Juan. More significantly, the dramatic tension created by suspicion and the subsequent self-interrogation are very like the situation in Tonight Is the Prelude. The mysterious, almost miraculous, arrival of the letter which provides Marina with the opportunity to save herself, also parallels Tonight Is the Prelude. The endings of both plays where the characters seek a correct moral answer and reconciliation with their spouses or friends are highly idealized.

A number of similarities also exist between The Lady Receives a Letter and works of other playwrights. Francisco Álvaro places the play in the line of Priestley's An Inspector Calls and Dangerous Corner, Alfonso Paso's Juicio contra un sinvergüenza [Judgment against a ne'er-do-well] and Cena de matrimonios [Dinner for married couples], and Casona's Las tres perfectas casadas [The three perfect wives].[38] The comparison with this latter play is particularly interesting. The Three Perfect Wives premièred in Buenos Aires in 1941 but was not staged in Spain until the 1965-66 season. In the Casona play, three couples are spending the evening together, awaiting the arrival of their friend, Gustavo. When Gustavo is believed to have died in an accident, they open a letter he left to be read by them in the event of his death. Gustavo confesses that he has had a love affair with all three of the wives. The tension this news creates between the husbands and wives is not unlike the situation in the Ruiz Iriarte play after the receipt of the anonymous note. In both cases, the letter has been read by mistake. In the Casona play, Gustavo was not aboard the plane that crashed. Although the Casona play ends tragically with the death of Gustavo—perhaps a suicide, perhaps killed by one of the wives—the plays are also similar in their use of a Pirandellian approach to levels of reality.

In general The Lady Receives a Letter has not received favorable critical attention. Holt, while finding fault with the title, does believe "the author demonstrates with fine dramatic skills that the line between reality and illusion is not easily recognized and that the truth is multiple, while bringing his characters to a more authentic understanding of their own special interrelationships." [39] More typically, however, critics have observed that the play is neither new in its techniques nor in what it reveals of human nature. As one of them has noted, the play's conflict, development and solution "could not be more conventional." [40] Nicolás González Ruiz probably put his finger on the play's greatest weakness when he stated that the "ending pleased the audience a great deal." [41] Initially the play promises to uncover deep psychological truths about the various characters, but ultimately we learn little about them that is profound. The value system of the middle-class audience is not shaken, and apparently all's well that ends well. Within the play Alberto anticipates this negative criticism when he comments that either an optimistic or a pessimistic ending opens a Spanish playwright to widespread criticism from one sector or another of society; the only way to please everyone is to be ambiguous. [42] In this case an ambiguous ending, like that of Casona's *The Three Perfect Wives*, might have enhanced the Pirandellian overtones of the play and placed the work among Ruiz Iriarte's more interesting treatments of the illusion-reality theme.

V Story of Adultery

It is indeed ambiguity with respect to appearance and reality that underscores the last of Ruiz Iriarte's serious plays, *Historia de un adulterio* [Story of adultery]. Starring Enrique Diosdado and Amelia de la Torre, the play opened in February, 1969. In many respects it returns to *The Carousel* in theatrical technique and in its critical view of high society. Francisco Alvaro is undoubtedly not alone in believing that these two plays are Ruiz Iriarte's most important works.[43] Holt has found the later play to be a mature drama and, from a structural point of view, the playwright's most complex work.[44] Certainly *Story of Adultery* represents Ruiz Iriarte's most ambitious use of flashbacks, the most innovative approach to the treatment of time, and the most explicit presentation of a Pirandellian relativity of truth.

The principal action of the play, like that of the other serious dramas, spans only a few hours. Ernesto Luján, an extremely powerful banker and businessman, experiences sudden pangs of conscience. He views with alarm the frivolous, superficial, snobbish woman that his wife Adelaida has become over the years. He is dismayed to find the same traits in Rosalía, the idealistic, decent

young woman who became his mistress some years before in order to
further her husband's career. He wonders if Jorge, Rosalía's husband,
knows to what he owes his phenomenal rise to success in the firm.
Disgusted with the person he has become himself and determined to
restore them all to their authentic selves, Ernesto decides to do away
with his image as a banker, give away all of his stock in his company,
and return to his beginnings. The other three think he has gone
insane. They have no desire to give up their power, their luxury, and
their carefree, frivolous lives. Ernesto resigns himself to the impossi-
bility of turning back the hands of time. He promises Adelaida a trip
to Paris, makes Jorge a vice president in the company, and allows the
status quo to continue.

The plot of the play is spare. Its dramatic interest lies in the
presentation of the story, not in the story itself. As the first act begins,
Ernesto has already informed the others of his intention to sell his
stock. Thinking he is mad, they have called the doctor. To the elderly
physician, an almost comic figure, Ernesto confesses his relationship
with Rosalía and relates through a series of flashbacks what had
transpired earlier in the evening. The doctor is then a spectator of
action which takes the form of a play within the play. Obviously the
flashback technique is somewhat related to the one used in *The
Carousel*, but the doctor here remains on the stage simultaneously
with the scenes from the recent past. Because of the two ongoing
levels of time, the doctor is treated like a ghost, invisible to the
characters reenacting the past. The flashbacks do not recount the
entire sequence of events in chronological order as did the flashbacks
in *Tonight Is the Prelude* or *The Carousel* but rather represent
selected moments to dramatize points Ernesto wishes to make. In the
second act, Adelaida, too, decides that she would like to confess to the
doctor what has happened. Ernesto now becomes one of the characters in the flashbacks for whom the doctor is invisible. The scene
Adelaida recalls in bringing to a conclusion the events from earlier
that evening thus unifies the two levels of time. The doctor witnesses
the outcome to the drama recounted for him in the two confessions in
the present. As the play ends and the other characters leave, Ernesto
and Adelaida are left with their thoughts of a more distant past
evoking the images of themselves when they first met and fell in love.

Ernesto finds in *Story of Adultery* that, in spite of his own deep
desire to right the wrongs that he has committed in the past, he is
unable to do so because of the self-interest of others. The theme is not
new to the Spanish theater. It forms the basic idea of Calvo-Sotelo's

La muralla [The wall, 1954] and of Echegaray's nineteenth-century play *O locura o santidad* [Madman or saint]. The theme also is not limited to Spain in its application although, once again, Ruiz Iriarte is apparently observing the changing moral values of his own country. Adelaida reveals to Ernesto that she has known all along that Rosalía is his mistress and that it simply does not matter. When they were first married, thirty years before, she had been deeply hurt by his infidelity but had concealed his illicit activities and her own feelings in order to protect his career: "In those days in Spain adultery was looked down upon, and your business would have suffered, I'm sure." [45] In the present, such concerns no longer matter. She and Rosalía are both accepted in the best social circles, including Church organizations. Rosalía's social triumph is directly related to her status as the mistress of a wealthy man. As Ernesto tells the doctor, "It turned out that everyone loved her and respected her more than ever" (*S*, 33). Like Diana in *The Grand Minuet*, Rosalía's status is dependent upon her love affair and she is corrupted by the power that derives from her relationship with an important man. Ruiz Iriarte's satirical view of Spanish society in *Story of Adultery* is, in fact, very much like his criticism of power and human weakness in *The Grand Minuet*; in both cases, the idealism of youth quickly dies.

In some respects *Story of Adultery* is the most Pirandellian of Ruiz Iriarte's plays. Here for the first time the Spanish playwright destroys the illusionism of the theater, making it clear that the scenes presented to us in the flashbacks are a spectacle deliberately evoked for the benefit of the doctor and the audience. The characters are manipulated at the whim first of Ernesto and then of Adelaida somewhat in the way Pirandello's characters direct the actors in *Six Characters in Search of an Author* to stage their drama from the past. More significantly, however, Ruiz Iriarte maintains throughout the play a certain ambiguity with respect to Jorge and Rosalía. Ernesto must know if Jorge knows the truth, for Ernesto's own guilt and responsibility are directly related to Jorge's knowledge. If Jorge accepts his wife's infidelity as a means of furthering his career, then Ernesto is being exploited by Jorge, not the reverse. If Jorge is innocent, then Ernesto is even more of a scoundrel than before. In spite of his repeated questioning of Jorge, Ernesto never gets a clearcut answer. He and the doctor vacillate. One scene makes them believe that Jorge does not know, but the next makes them think the opposite. Jorge speaks of Rosalía's love and her importance to him. He is ambitious because he wants everything for her. "For her I would be capable of anything" (S, 52). Jorge says that he does not want to know (S, 74); but he also affirms that those who are envious of him spread vicious rumors about his wife (S, 81). At the end, Ernesto and the doctor conclude that they will never be sure whether Jorge knows of his wife's infidelity or not.

Quite obviously Jorge's attitude toward truth is Pirandellian. Truth is relative, and Jorge's happiness results from his belief in an acceptable reality. More subtle is the possibility that Rosalía, too, functions on a different level of reality than that envisioned by Ernesto. When we first see her, she chides Ernesto for missing their weekly tryst and expresses feelings of jealousy. But does she really care about him? In later scenes, she evinces affection for Jorge, declaring at one point that he will never understand everything that she is capable of doing for him (S, 82). Ernesto may believe that she is his loving mistress when in truth she continues to sacrifice herself for the man she really loves, Jorge. Jorge in turn may know of her sacrifice and accept it because it is the only way in which he can provide her with the kind of life he feels she deserves. Beyond the level of illusion in which Ernesto feigns fidelity for his wife and friendship for Jorge may be another level of illusion in which Rosalía feigns love for Ernesto and Jorge feigns friendship for his employer.

Although *Story of Adultery* is generally accepted as one of Ruiz Iriarte's best plays, critics have cited two particular aspects as defects. The next-to-last scene, with its flashback of the youthful Ernesto and Adelaida, is considered to be both unnecessary and unduly sentimental.[46] At the least, the scene does break the unity of the play in the sense that all of the other action takes place during the same evening. On the other hand, within the context of a play where scenes from the past may be evoked through the conscience of the main characters, the visualization of Ernesto and Adelaida's thoughts is not unexpected. This "sentimental epilogue" has also been criticized for creating the impression that the problem presented in the first act has been evaded.[47] Indeed it has—and that in part is Ruiz Iriarte's point. In contemporary Spanish society, materialism is so much more powerful than spiritual or moral values that such problems cannot be solved.

The ending of the play is also consistent with Ruiz Iriarte's underlying philosophical theme. López Sancho has noted that there is something Sartrean about *Story of Adultery*.[48] Ruiz Iriarte has not attempted to develop philosophical concepts in any of his other plays, but in this case there is a slight tendency toward existentialism.

Ernesto has experienced a kind of existentialist awakening, "a crisis of anguish and remorse" (S, 63). It is for this reason that he seeks someone outside himself who will listen as he seeks his authentic self. He tells the doctor that by chance he will be "the other" (S, 15). Madness, he later says, may be the "arrival of the other" (S, 78), that is the search for the authentic self. Following his probing of his inner self and of his life, Ernesto experiences something akin to Sartrean nausea: "Everything around me fills me with loathing!" he tells Adelaida (S, 63). He offers to Jorge the chance to begin again, "to be free" but Jorge rejects freedom (S, 64-65). Ultimately Ernesto realizes that no one can begin again and that he must accept the responsibility for his past acts which have, in fact, created the person he is. "The punishment is in continuing, in having to continue in spite of everything; onward, always onward, come what may" (S, 77). Ernesto's conclusion is not unlike that of Sartre's characters in *Huis clos* [No exit] when they realize that they themselves are hell and that therefore there is no escape. In the final scene, when Ernesto and Adelaida have evoked their former selves, they realize that they are responsible for their own destinies and their own personalities. It is from the contrast between what they were and what they have become that Adelaida cries out to Ernesto the closing lines, "What have we done?" (S, 88).

Story of Adultery is a well constructed play, demonstrating Ruiz Iriarte's usual skill as a craftsman but this time in a more complex structure. It is also his most profound play and perhaps the most fully developed and interesting treatment of the illusion-reality theme. It stands with *The Carousel* as evidence that the master writer of comedies is equally adept at handling serious drama.

CHAPTER 7

The Television Plays

ON January 1, 1966, *Televisión Española* (TVE) broadcast the first in a series of half-hour original comedies written by Ruiz Iriarte. On successive Saturday evenings that year, his *La pequeña comedia* [Little theater] aired thirty-four dramas. The series subsequently was awarded the National Television Prize. Since that beginning more than a decade ago, Ruiz Iriarte has written over one hundred television plays and has come to consider this aspect of his literary career as one of major importance. In the introduction to their student edition of three of Ruiz Iriarte's television plays, Marion P. Holt and George W. Woodyard observe that Ruiz Iriarte's *Little Theater* coincides with the development of local television production in Spain.[1] When regular television transmissions began in 1956, most of the programs shown on TVE were imported from other countries. Starting in the 1960s, however, Spain not only produced her own television films but began exporting them to other Spanish-speaking nations. Local productions have included television versions of *zarzuelas* (Spanish opera), classic Spanish drama, and more recent theatrical successes of such contemporary playwrights as Buero Vallejo, López Rubio and Mihura. The popularity of dramatic presentations also encouraged some established playwrights to prepare scripts expressly for the new medium.

Long a defender of popular theater, Ruiz Iriarte has also become a proponent of television plays as a literary genre. In the prologue to his anthology of *Little Theater*, he reminds his readers that at one time motion pictures were regarded as a pastime for illiterates but that today we recognize cinema as a valid form of literary and artistic expression.[2] Moreover, he notes, television reaches a large, diversified audience, far greater and more varied than that for legitimate theater. "I am sure, very sure, that none of my stage plays, not even those most favored by fortune, reached as large an audience as any one of these 'little comedies' " (*L*, 10).

Familiar with the techniques of the theater and of motion pictures,

Ruiz Iriarte finds that television bears a relationship to both of them but at the same time remains unique. Television plays require a "different rhythm" than either stage plays or motion pictures and the scripts written for one medium cannot be presented in another without substantial revision. "But, nevertheless, television has something of theater—the ancient, eternal, irreplaceable 'dramatic situation'—and quite a bit of cinema: its free and easy narrative, its similar manner of 'telling' the story, its playing with time, its jumping from scene to scene" (*L*, 11). Television incorporates the noble and lofty demands of theater with the fresh and impetuous charm of motion pictures (*L*, 12). The playwright acknowledges that writing a play a week placed an enormous strain on him but affirms that he approached the task with joy and spontaneity (*L*, 12).

Quite obviously the television plays do differ in technique from Ruiz Iriarte's stage plays. He makes use of occasional panoramic scenes, changes of location, sound effects, and off-camera voices that would not lend themselves easily to stage productions. On the other hand, the changes of scene are relatively limited and most settings are inside locations, easier to film within the restrictions of the medium than motion picture scripts tend to be. Ruiz Iriarte has often stated that a playwright must learn his trade; the same wisdom holds true for the writer of television plays where, once again, Ruiz Iriarte has proved himself a skilled craftsman.

As literature, the television plays are brief, compact works, more closely related to short stories and one-act plays than to full-length comedies. Working within the half-hour time limit, the playwright has had to introduce his characters and situations and develop his theme with the greatest possible economy of words and actions. Accepting the challenge these limitations present, Ruiz Iriarte has succeeded in creating vivid scenes and characters that remain etched in the memory of the reader or viewer.

In many ways the short television comedies resemble Ruiz Iriarte's stage plays. Several of them are works of poetic fantasy, like his early theater, and many of them include the kind of gentle satire of contemporary society that we have seen throughout his career. In general optimistic plays, showing the best of human nature, they are quite suitable for family viewing. As is true with his literary production as a whole, he avoids political and economic problems. His characters tend to be of the middle-class, but he rejects the identification of happiness with affluence. Rather, he continues to criticize an overemphasis on material possessions and "success" while repeating his familiar message that love and understanding are more important than wealth or power. Certain recurring themes in the television comedies—the effort to recapture the past, the search for happiness, the problems arising in interpersonal relationships—may be used as the basis for grouping the published plays to facilitate a closer examination of them.

I   *In Search of the Past*

The first play in Ruiz Iriarte's television series, *"Milady," Objetos para regalos* ["Milady," Gift Shop], introduced a theme that was to reappear with variations not only in several of the other short comedies but also in his major stage productions of 1967 and 1968. One of the characters in the play, the stranger, has returned to Spain after a number of years in exile. He comes to the old neighborhood and looks for the store where the girl he loved worked. The store apparently is gone, and the lively young clerks in the fancy gift shop that has taken its place know nothing about the past or the woman he seeks. Gradually they realize that their employer, Doña Cecilia, in fact is the stranger's lost love, and they bring the couple together. The two do not appear to know each other, however, and the stranger goes on his way. "Why didn't they recognize each other?" asks one of the clerks. "Don't you know? Because, in truth, each of them was in love with a dream," replies another (*L*, 43).

Ruiz Iriarte's character hopes to recapture the past but finds that the years have changed Spain and all that he had remembered. For him it is impossible to erase the thirty years of exile. The confrontation of the stranger and Doña Cecilia is reminiscent of a famous one-act play by the Álvarez Quintero brothers *Mañana de sol* [Sunny morning, 1905], based in turn on a nineteenth century poem of Campoamor:

> Twenty years pass: he returns,
> and on seeing each other, they exclaim:
> ("Good heavens! Is that he?")
> ("Good God! Can that be she?")

Ruiz Iriarte's setting is contemporary Madrid and the particular circumstances of the stranger's return are rooted in the historical moment, but the essential dramatic situation is unquestionably universal.

In *"Milady," Gift Shop* Ruiz Iriarte treats with a certain nostalgia a past which can never be recaptured. He evokes that past in part through music of the earlier period, much as he did in *An Umbrella Under the Rain*. In *El café* [The cafe] it is the setting itself that evokes the past. In several of his essays, including his four-part memoirs, the playwright has written with fondness of the old-style cafe where young authors might gather to discuss their work and where friends might meet every afternoon or evening to pass leisurely hours in conversation. In postwar Madrid the old cafes have rapidly been replaced by *cafeterías*, modern coffee shops very different in their furnishings and in their atmosphere. In *The Cafe*, one of the old establishments, opened in 1910, will be closed forever the following morning. The old waiter is reminiscing about a particular group of students who used to congregate there years before when they begin one by one to arrive to bid farewell to the *Gran Café de Oriente*. In this reunion as in *"Milady," Gift Shop* it is readily apparent that the past cannot be recaptured. Four of the five men who return are now successful in their various fields but have little in common. Teresa long ago gave up her music and her ambitions. Jerónimo, the failure in the group, is left alone at the end, knowing that the six of them will never meet again in spite of their promises to one another to renew old acquaintances.

In *"Milady," Gift Shop* Ruiz Iriarte contrasts the attitudes of the stranger and Doña Cecilia with those of the three young salesgirls. In *The Cafe* he similarly juxtaposes the two generations. Three young reporters entering the cafe overhear the conversation of Teresa and her five male friends from student days. She admits that she had secretly loved one of them but will not reveal which. Marylín, one of the young people, cannot understand why a woman would keep her love secret rather than declare herself to the man. It is a theme Ruiz Iriarte has frequently developed in his comedies of manners. Women need no longer sit back passively and wait for the man to make the first move.

In *Cándida* the playwright once again presents a gathering of middle-aged men who are brought together by a memory from the past. In this case the television comedy bears a certain resemblance to *The Six-Horse Landau*, for the men are brought together by phone calls inviting them to dinner. The calls are from Cándida, with whom each of the men—quite surprised to find rivals present upon arriving at the announced address—had some twenty-five years before been in love. Although they are all successful in their fields—a famous actor, a famous banker, and a publishing scholar—all three reveal that they are lonely. When the mysterious Cándida finally arrives, she is an eighteen-year-old girl, the daughter of their Cándida from the past. Knowing that she herself was about to die, Cándida's mother had thought of her old friends as possible protectors for her soon-to-be orphaned child and had instructed the young Cándida to arrange the dinner after her death. At first all three men are offended and leave. They had hoped to recapture a lost love from the past and instead find themselves cast in the role of foster father. One by one, however, they each return, and the play ends on a comic note as the three fight over the privilege of adopting Cándida. Ruiz Iriarte's message here, as on many other occasions, is that love is the antidote for loneliness and hence also the key to happiness. The realization on the part of the three men of how they might benefit from becoming Cándida's guardian is very similar to the feeling of Laura for Cris in *The Flowers Cafe* or of the idealistic young couples for the elderly people they help in *Suicide Bridge* or *The Six-Horse Landau*. Ruiz Iriarte views love and charity on a very altruistic level, suggesting that those who give of themselves to others will reap spiritual rewards.

Somewhat related to the three television comedies discussed above is *Un ramo de rosas* [A bouquet of roses]. As in *"Milady," Gift Shop*, the setting is a store and the plot revolves around a man who has just returned to Madrid. In this case, the store is a florist shop and the stranger is Alfredo, a young man who has been in South Africa for three years. He buys the bouquet of roses for his sweetheart, only to learn that she is getting married that same day to someone else. The clash between past and present is handled on a farcical plane and without the nostalgia present in the other plays. At one point the whole wedding party invades the florist shop, creating an inevitable confrontation between the jealous bridegroom and the jilted boyfriend. Alfredo rises to the occasion, however, and indicates that he does understand why his girl did not patiently await his return. The wedding party leaves, and the comedy ends with the salesclerk suggesting that Alfredo take her out to lunch.

II   *In Search of Happiness*

In one of Ruiz Iriarte's early plays, *The Apprentice Lover*, Andrés concluded that happiness was to be found in quiet companionship and simple pleasures. The same basic message recurs twenty years later in the television comedies. *Un revuelo de palomas* [A flock of pigeons] is a satire of the consumer society. One of the two characters, the director, is oblivious to reality, including the fact that his secretary is in love with him, and spends his time dictating a paper in which he equates happiness with numbers of refrigerators, cars, etc. When he inadvertently notices that it is spring, however, he also realizes that his secretary is beautiful and suggests that they go to the park.

The five men in *El buscador de maravillas* [The seeker of miracles] similarly realize that they may have already achieved happiness. A diversified group, ranging in age from thirty to over fifty, the men meet once a month to play poker. On this particular evening a beautiful young woman suddenly enters the room from the balcony. The men think she loves one of them, but later learn that she is a thief. Nevertheless, as Gustavo, an optimistic bachelor playwright, points out to them, miracles do exist. Each of them has something to be thankful for—a loving wife, a loving son, etc.

Gustavo, who may represent Ruiz Iriarte himself, somewhat resembles the title figure of *Amador, el optimista* [Amador, the optimist], one of the best and most fanciful of the television comedies. Amador, an engineer, has just bought an apartment in a new building on the distant outskirts of Madrid. His next-door neighbor is Adela, an artist who had fallen in love with the former owner of the apartment. Adela reveals to Amador that she and her friends are pessimists who worry about the serious problems of life; Amador rejects this view. Life may be filled with disasters, but it is also filled with love and illusion. If one retains hope, then life is a stroll in a rose garden. Amador wins Adela over with the help of three friends who come for the housewarming: Paloma, a young girl who sells flowers; Saturnino, an old man who sells balloons; and Jerónimo, a beggar who plays the accordion and pretends to be blind. Amador's world is one of poetic fantasy. His whimsical friends are not unlike the strangers who invade the hotel room of Dionisio on the eve of his wedding in Mihura's *Tres sombreros de copa* [Three top hats, written in 1932 and staged in 1952]. Whereas in the Mihura play Dionisio must return to the unpleasant reality of the middle-class marriage that awaits him, Amador has rejected middle-class morality. He asks Adela to marry him and join him and his friends in their happiness. The flowers, balloons, and accordion music are all symbolic of the plane of illusion which Amador and the others have created as their own.

There is also an element of poetic fantasy in *El presidente y la felicidad* [The president and happiness] but blended with a satire of modern society. Valentín is a poor but happy language teacher who raises birds and lives modestly with his daughter. He receives a mysterious invitation to dine in the most elegant suite of an expensive hotel and finds himself in a surreal environment of high finance. The President and his assistants are constantly on the phone, buying and selling large blocks of stocks in all the major markets of the world. The atmosphere is farcical. Ultimately Valentín learns that the President, who is now the richest man in Europe, is lonely and unhappy and would gladly change places with the language teacher. Valentín, realizing that he would lose in such an exchange, slips out of the suite unnoticed and goes home. Although the tone of *The President and Happiness* is that of light comedy, the play does in some ways relate to the serious dramas Ruiz Iriarte was writing in the 1960s. Valentín serves as a witness from the outside to the affluent world of the President, much as the commissioner and the doctor do in *The Carousel* and *Story of Adultery*. And the President, like the successful businessmen of those two works, is unable to escape from his reality.

Also related to one of the serious dramas in structure and theme is *Sala de espera* [The waiting room]. Similar to *Tonight Is the Prelude*, Ruiz Iriarte brings together a group of travelers who must wait for their train to be repaired. The unexpected stopover gives the main character, the famous physicist Professor Cantini, the opportunity to reconsider the trip he is making to Paris. The playwright adds a new dimension to *The Waiting Room*, however, for Cantini falls asleep and imagines a group of travelers who have all just died and are seated together awaiting the last judgment. His dream is precipitated by his reading the obituary notices of Larry-Loop, a clown who fell off a tight rope; Madame Flor, a greedy woman who was killed by thieves; Mademoiselle Berta, a millionaire's daughter who dies in an automobile accident; the pleasure loving Prince of Wigsburd-Badem, who was assassinated; and the student, who was shot down after he killed the Prince. The situation is like that of López Rubio's *La otra orilla* [The other shore, 1954], both because one of the characters is actually alive and because at first the others do not realize they are dead. In Cantini's dream, the deceased all realize with regret that they wasted their lives and must face the last judgment with heavy burdens of guilt. The physicist, who was en route to Paris to deliver his secret formula for a highly destructive bomb, awakens, burns his papers, and returns home. In his dream he has learned that there is a God. With this knowledge he has regained hope and no longer wants any part in the modern technology of war.

III   *Interpersonal Relationships*

A strong religious theme also marks *El secreto* [The secret], a television comedy that develops once again Ruiz Iriarte's familiar concern for the generation gap. Ernestina and Vicente, like the parents in *The Carousel*, are an affluent couple, caught up in their social life and oblivious to the real concerns of their daughter Martita. They are thus very startled when she confronts them at three o'clock in the morning and announces that she plans to become a nun. "I am very conservative and very, very Catholic. But no daughter of mine is going to be a nun," exclaims her mother (*L*, 260). Martita runs away but is brought back home by Sor Catalina, a young nun who convinces Vicente through her example that Martita, not her parents, may have found the secret to happiness. "Do you believe that we have found any meaning to life?" he asks his wife (*L*, 268). Ruiz Iriarte both satirizes the hypocrisy of the mother and suggests overtly here, as he had done only indirectly in *The Carousel*, that life without faith is empty and superficial.

In *El collar* [The necklace], Ruiz Iriarte develops a conflict among friends somewhat similar to the one in *The Lady Receives a Letter* and also shows once again the negative effect of materialism. Three couples, who have been friends for years, are to dine out together in celebration of Rosalía's birthday. As a present, Rosalía's husband Eduardo, now a wealthy businessman, has bought her a necklace worth a million *pesetas*. The other two couples are less affluent than Eduardo and Rosalía but undoubtedly happier. When Rosalía's necklace disappears during dinner, Eduardo accuses the others of having stolen it. Although it is later found by the waiter on the terrace where Rosalía had lost it, the damage has already been done and the friendship destroyed. Eduardo knows that he was wrong to have lost faith in his companions and to have placed a higher value on the necklace than on their friendship, but his realization comes too late.

In a more lighthearted vein Ruiz Iriarte deals once again with the topic of marital conflicts in *La fuga* [The flight]. Three husbands who wish to escape from their wives make up the story that they must go to Switzerland on business. Instead they rent a house outside Madrid just to get away from home. At first in their new-found tranquility they discover that they have nothing to talk about, but gradually they start to discuss their spouses. They quickly convince each other that their wives are wonderful and decide to go home. At home, in keeping with the tradition of farce, the wives quickly display all the same flaws in character that forced the husbands to flee in the first place.

Aimed more directly at one of the annoyances of contemporary life in Spain, *El piso* [The apartment] deals with the housing crisis. Amador in *Amador, the Optimist* had pointed out that his new home was so far outside Madrid that it would take him two hours to get to the Puerta del Sol. Nicolás in *The Apartment* cannot get married because he and María have not been able to find a place to live at all. He is therefore delighted when an old classmate promises to rent him an apartment. Unfortunately, the classmate's wife has promised the same apartment to Magdalena, who has been unable to marry Félix because they, too, have no place to live. When the two couples converge on the apartment at the same time, initially the two women begin to fight. But María and Magdalena develop a strong mutual sympathy and each decides that the other needs the apartment more. Their potential sacrifice is in vain, however, for Nicolás learns that the apartment has been rented to a foreigner who was willing to pay five times as much as the Spaniards could afford. He suggests to Félix that they not tell the women the truth so that each of them may retain the illusion that she has done something to bring happiness to the other.

The published television comedies, like Ruiz Iriarte's stage plays, range from farce (*The Flight, The Bouquet of Roses*) to serious drama (*The Necklace*), with the majority of them falling within the range of comedy. The background for the *Little Theater* is predominantly Madrid, not only because this is the locale where the series was filmed but because the capital city has almost always been the scene Ruiz Iriarte has chosen for his literary works. The characters, too, are familiar, with the *pobrecito* figure from the earlier comedies of manners reappearing in *Amador, the Optimist* and *The President and Happiness* and the successful but lonely businessman of the later serious dramas represented in *The President and Happiness* and *The Secret*.

In spite of the similarities in tone, setting, and characterization, the television comedies differ somewhat from the stage plays in their themes. Although Ruiz Iriarte is not overtly moralistic in either of the two genres, in the television plays, perhaps because of their greater intensity, his thoughts on some issues are presented more clearly or with a greater sense of immediacy than in the longer plays. The religious theme, for example, which is only hinted at in *Tonight Is the Prelude* or *The Carousel* is highlighted in *The Waiting Room* and *The Secret*. The criticism of the meaningless existence of the affluent, although directly stated in *The Carousel, The Lady Receives a Letter*, and *Story of Adultery*, is satirized even more forcefully in some of the television comedies. In *The President and Happiness*, the world of high finance is shown on a plane of absurdity, and in *A Flock of Pigeons*, the ideal of the consumer society is held up to ridicule. Ruiz Iriarte evokes the past with affection and points out that the technological progress of the present does not necessarily represent an improvement. Certainly his satire is aimed at *urbanización*, the development of high-rise apartments on the outskirts of the city (*Amador, the Optimist*), and at the use of science to destroy human life (*The Waiting Room*). His television comedies may not emphasize the problems of the poor or elements of social conflict, but they do constantly question the values of the middle-class in postwar Spain.

Particularly interesting when placed in the trajectory of Ruiz Iriarte's total literary production is the evolution of the *pobrecito* character in the television comedies. In his early plays, the *pobrecito* was a lonely individual, often rejected by others because he did not conform to society's expectations. His wife and family or his potential spouse criticized him for not being successful, for not being able to buy the things his family wanted, or for not being a romantic Don Juan figure. In the plays of the 1960s, the *pobrecito* is largely replaced by the successful man who has conformed but now finds himself lonely and alienated because he can neither accept the person he has become nor return to his authentic self. In the television comedies, Ruiz Iriarte again presents examples of the *pobrecito*—this time no longer necessarily a lonely nonconformist. Instead, he may be surrounded by loving family—Valentín in *The President and Happiness*—or friends—Amador. When Ruiz Iriarte juxtaposes the two characters in *The President and Happiness* it becomes clear that the *pobrecito* is no longer an antihero but rather the object of envy on the part of the "successful" businessman. When one sells one's soul to the gods of materialism, power and wealth, there is no possibility for happiness.

Perhaps more obviously than in his stage plays as a whole, in the television comedies Ruiz Iriarte stresses the importance of happiness and optimism. In the best of the television scripts, he gives full rein to his poetic fantasy, utilizing the possibilities of the medium for the presentation of varying levels of illusion and reality. The result is a dramatic series of unquestionable literary value, certainly superior to much of the original television programming done in the United States in recent years.

CHAPTER 8

The Later Comedies

IN 1958 with *Tonight Is the Prelude*, Ruiz Iriarte introduced a series of plays which, while they continued to use certain elements of comedy, are obviously more serious in tone and intent than the majority of his works. Simultaneously, however, in the decade of the 1960s, he continued to create comedies, including two that are among his most important and successful plays. *Tengo un millón* [I have a million], staged in 1960, is a detective comedy, closely related to a number of Spanish and foreign works that were very popular in Spain during the period. It is also related to two of Ruiz Iriarte's own comedies of the late 1950s which were not among his best theater and which he has chosen to leave unpublished.

In 1967, after the triumphs of the serious *The Carousel* and the theatrical game *An Umbrella Under the Rain*, Ruiz Iriarte turned once again to comedy and staged the highly successful *La muchacha del sombrerito rosa* [The girl in the little pink hat] and its sequel *Primavera en la Plaza de París* [Springtime in the Plaza de París]. These two plays deal with a liberal intellectual who returns to his native land and his wife after almost thirty years in exile. Although the two plays are closely related in plot, the first may appropriately be termed high comedy while the second, much lighter in tone, does not include the same psychological development of its characters.

Following *Story of Adultery* in 1969, Ruiz Iriarte wrote no new original stage plays until 1975. *Buenas noches, Sabina* [Good evening, Sabina], which enjoyed a run of more than one hundred performances, centers on a theme of marital infidelity. Both in terms of its characters and its plot, it is somewhat reminiscent of the comedies of manners of the 1950s.

I I Have a Million

A comedy of minor importance in Ruiz Iriarte's total theater, *Tengo un millón* [I have a million] was staged in the winter of 1960 by

actor-director Adolfo Marsillach. Chronologically the play falls between two of Ruiz Iriarte's relative failures—*A Private Investigation*
and *De París viene mamá* [Mama's coming from Paris]—neither of
which has been published. Apparently *I Have a Million* has some
elements in common with the two other comedies as well as with
Tonight Is the Prelude (1958), particularly with respect to its use of
stock "detective story" devices. *I Have a Million* takes place in a
modest apartment on the outskirts of Madrid, one of the distant
developments Ruiz Iriarte was to satirize later in the television
comedy *Amador, the Optimist*. Mateo, the main character, once
again is a *pobrecito*, but this time one worried about his low income
and rising debts. His wife Patricia loves him, but she, too, is preoccupied by their financial situation. On his way home from work—Mateo
takes the subway, a trolley, a bus, and then walks for a half-hour—he
sees a pedestrian hit by a car and discovers a bag of money by the
accident victim's side. Inspired by the detective stories he has seen in
the movies, he switches identification with the man he presumes to
be dead and takes the million *pesetas*.[1] His intention is to pretend to
be dead and to escape to France with Patricia by using the passport he
has stolen.

   In developing this basic situation, the playwright uses a number of
farcical techniques. The superstitious maid believes that Mateo is a
ghost. Mateo hides from time to time in a closet, as do the other
characters who rapidly enter the scene as complication follows complication. As the action progresses, we learn that the dead pedestrian
is alive and well and that he is an underworld figure who looks and
talks like a conservative businessman. He has stolen the million
pesetas from Roberto, who in turn had taken the money from a widow
on the pretense of using it to start a business when in fact he had
intended to flee to France with a nightclub dancer. The widow herself
had stolen the money from the trust fund of her fourteen-year-old
daughter in order to give it to her lover. Mateo initially concludes that
everyone is dishonest so that he might as well keep the money; but
when little Marita arrives, saying that her mother told her that Mateo
and Patricia have something that belongs to her, Mateo softens and
returns the money to its rightful owner. Patricia and Mateo will
remain poor, but they will be free from guilt.

   The conclusion of the comedy, like the ending of *Tonight Is the
Prelude*, is optimistic, at least with respect to the morally correct
decision of Mateo and Patricia. But most of the comedy is farcical in
tone, with no overtly serious purpose. Ruiz Iriarte reveals each new

complication sequentially, so that the audience as well as Patricia and Mateo must unravel the mysteries one by one. He exploits to the fullest the comic potential in mistaken identities, comic irony, and inverted roles. The action of the play moves quickly with a rapid succession of entrances and exits, as the various characters come and go, hiding sometimes in the closet, sometimes in the other rooms of the apartment. The comedy is clearly designed to hold the attention of the audience and to entertain.

As mentioned in Chapter Six, detective stories were in vogue on the Spanish stage in the late 1950s. Ruiz Iriarte was not unaware of the trend. *A Private Investigation* and *Tonight Is the Prelude* were both related to the subgenre, and *Mama's Coming from Paris* also included a subplot relating to the kleptomania of some of the characters.[2] Mateo's moral dilemma in *I Have a Million* is a more extensive treatment of the situation of Valentín in *Tonight Is the Prelude*, while Roberto's betrayal of the widow is not unlike the deception of Rosa by Javier in the earlier play. In all of these plays Ruiz Iriarte cleverly unravels mysteries and identifies the guilty parties.

It is also during the period of the late 1950s that the playwright shows a repeated interest in the situation of widows and widowers, including the problems faced by their children. The theme is present not only in *I Have a Million* but also in *The Private Life of Mama, Tonight Is the Prelude*, and *Mama's Coming from Paris*. In the latter comedy, the young daughters must adjust to a French stepmother. In two of Ruiz Iriarte's most successful comedies from the late 1960s, *The Girl in the Little Pink Hat* and *Springtime in the Plaza de París*, the playwright deals with a similar but somewhat more complicated situation.

II The Girl in the Little Pink Hat

La muchacha del sombrerito rosa [The girl in the little pink hat] and its sequel *Primavera en la Plaza de París* [Springtime in the Plaza de París], two of Ruiz Iriarte's most successful comedies, were written and staged between *The Carousel* and *Story of Adultery*, his two most important works of serious intent. These four plays together represent the culmination of the playwright's career to date.

The Girl in the Little Pink Hat opened in Madrid in April, 1967, and continued into the 1967-68 theatrical season as well. Starring Amelia de la Torre and Enrique Diosdado, the play won for Ruiz

Iriarte the National Literature Prize of 1967. As the playwright notes in his self-criticism, the basic situation of *The Girl in the Little Pink Hat* is one which related very closely to the contemporary reality of Spain.[3] In the 1960s it became possible for those who had favored the losing side in the Civil War to return from exile. Many well known writers and scholars chose to do so. Alejandro Casona, for example, who visited Spain in 1962, subsequently resided there permanently from 1963 until his death in 1965. In Ruiz Iriarte's comedy, Esteban Lafuente, a liberal intellectual who had left Spain in March, 1939, returns in triumph in 1967. His lecture at the Ateneo is greeted by a large and enthusiastic audience, and TVE announces that he is a source of national pride. On the personal level, however, his situation is not so clear. Twenty-eight years before he had abandoned his wife Leonor, the daughter of a respected conservative family. The action of the play revolves around her response first to his sudden reappearance and then to the knowledge that he is accompanied by three teenage daughters.

In one sense the basic dramatic situation in *The Girl in the Little Pink Hat* is as old and as universal as the myth of Ulysses and Penelope. In another sense, however, the comedy is essentially Spanish and must be viewed in that context. Leonor, very clearly the central figure in the action, incarnates traditional Spanish values but with an admirable willingness to adjust to contemporary reality. Sainz de Robles is quite correct in suggesting that the play might have been called *The Portrait of a Lady*.[4] Initially Leonor had not accompanied her husband into exile in spite of her deep love for him because her sense of duty was greater. Torn between honor and love like Jimena in Guillén de Castro's Golden Age drama *Las mocedades del Cid* [The young Cid], Leonor had remained true to her family name and her heritage. When she learned that Esteban was living in Buenos Aires with another woman, she declared him "dead" and maintained her dignity, but she never ceased to love or consider herself married to him. In truth, she was his legitimate wife and as a Spanish woman raised in the Catholic religion would so consider herself.[5] In remaining faithful to him during his long years of absence, she has, in essence, remained faithful to herself and to her upbringing. Unlike the female protagonists of some of Ruiz Iriarte's earlier comedies of manners, she has not been confused by changing standards of behavior because her own moral values have proved stronger than loneliness or temptation. But unlike the stereotypical image of the abandoned woman in Spanish literature, she has also not retreated from the world or escaped into madness.[6] Leonor is undoubtedly the most complex and the most fully developed female character in Ruiz Iriarte's theater.

The setting of the play is Leonor's elegant nineteenth-century home on the Plaza de París in Madrid. The choice of locale is intended both to reinforce the portrait of Leonor as a traditional, conservative woman and to lend credence to Esteban's nostalgia for his beloved city and homeland. The ambience once again is that of the upper middle-class, but the Plaza de París is far removed from the new high-rise apartments or suburban chalets that Ruiz Iriarte sometimes uses for background. Esteban has found much that is new in Spain, but the house where he lived as a newlywed and the church of the Salesas where he was married have remained unchanged. What he does not anticipate, however, is that Leonor is also essentially unchanged by the passage of time.

Ruiz Iriarte displays his usual skillful craftsmanship in the presentation of his characters and story. As the play opens, Esteban enters the room and is greeted by Damián, an elderly servant. This scene of exposition is interrupted by the entrance of Leonor and Lola, causing Esteban to hide. Lola is a younger woman, very much representative of the kind of frivolous, amoral person the playwright frequently satirizes. Lola serves as a foil to Leonor, and their conversation thus quickly establishes Leonor's character and her fidelity to Esteban both for the audience and for him. In the obligatory scene between husband and wife which follows, Ruiz Iriarte develops with masterful sensitivity the psychological reaction of Leonor to Esteban's return. Her initial attitude towards him quite understandably changes when she learns that his mistress had died five years before—but reverses again when the three daughters, Marita, Paloma and Belén, reveal themselves.

In the second act, Marita comes to see Leonor. She feels obliged to tell her something about Belén, the mother of the three girls. From the young woman, Leonor learns that Belén, who shared Leonor's traditional values, had never been completely happy in her situation. She had met Esteban on the ship carrying them both into exile and had saved him from suicide. She had been his hope in a time of despair, but their liaison had filled her with remorse. Moreover Esteban's life abroad had been one of instability, as he had traveled from country to country, teaching at one university after another in South America and the United States. "Why is life so difficult?" asks Leonor. "Why is there always another truth?" (*M*, 46). With great compassion, Leonor understands that Esteban and Belén suffered over the years just as she herself had.[7] As the two younger sisters enter, she finds herself charmed by all three girls. Much to Esteban's surprise, she invites them to go with her to Paris for a few days and, upon their return, insists that they come to live with her. When she realizes that Esteban might fall prey to Lola if left on his own, she also welcomes him into her home—as a guest if not a husband.

Ruiz Iriarte introduces a number of his usual comic devices and characters into *The Girl in the Little Pink Hat*. Damián, the old servant, is a comic figure, as were the elderly servants in some of the earlier comedies. The lively teenagers once again stand in comic contrast to the older generation. Lola is a caricature, and her lines in particular are filled with double meanings. In that the audience is aware of the presence of Esteban and his three daughters before Leonor is, there is also ample opportunity for the playwright to exploit the comic irony in this situation. *The Girl in the Little Pink Hat* is nevertheless high comedy, with less use of farcical techniques and better developed characters than in the light comedies of manners. Esteban, although lacking the depth of characterization of Leonor, is also basically a dignified, noble figure; he is portrayed as a man who left his wife and country not for frivolous reasons but because of his sincere beliefs and the political reality of the moment. If he lacks Leonor's intuition about people, that is not so much an individual failing as proof of her contention that men "never understand anything" (*M*, 59).

According to the playwright's self-criticism, *The Girl in the Little Pink Hat* is a "love story with its past and its present, its nostalgia and its hope" (*M*, 5). To a large extent, that love is the affection Leonor feels for the three girls, who presently are, or under her tutelage will become, as Madrilenian as their names.[8] Like Laura in *The Flowers Cafe*, Leonor regrets not having had children of her own and is more than willing to adopt the motherless girls. It is the message Ruiz Iriarte has repeated throughout his theater: the cure for loneliness lies in giving generously of oneself to others. As she explains to Esteban when convincing him to give her his daughters, "Besides, the girls love me, you know. I don't know why. Perhaps because affection is, sometimes, a miracle. A beautiful and mysterious miracle. Perhaps because they feel alone and need someone to love them" (*M*, 73). Leonor's love also extends to Esteban. She knows that she will be criticized for having him live with her but she feels strong in her own moral convictions, which spring from the heart. "My friends will talk about me and yours will say terrible things. But what difference can it make to us? What we do we do for love. That love that forgives, forgets and hopes" (*M*, 83).

Underlying the drama of Leonor and Esteban as individuals is, of course, the symbolic application of their story to Spain itself. There is undoubtedly some validity in Holt's observation that the play and its sequel are sentimental and that in showing the softening and mellowing of political convictions by the passage of time, Ruiz Iriarte was telling his public what it wanted to hear.[9] But what he was telling them was also substantially true. Leonor astutely observes that Esteban, a liberal of the old school, may find that he is a conservative in contemporary Spain (*M*, 27).[10] The audience at his lecture is dominantly of the affluent middle-class, and his own daughters say that his political views are hopelessly antiquated. His comment that young Spaniards laugh at the older generation who divided the world into left and right is certainly not unfounded (*M*, 69). Leonor's acceptance of her husband's illegitimate daughters may be an exceptional case, but many children of exiled Spaniards have received warm welcomes from their relatives in Spain.

III Springtime in the Plaza de París

The political implications of *The Girl in the Little Pink Hat* are developed more extensively in the sequel play. *Springtime in the Plaza de París* also starred Amelia de la Torre and Enrique Diosdado and opened in Madrid in the winter of 1968. It was subsequently awarded the María Rolland prize. In the second comedy, Ruiz Iriarte satirizes the members of the older generation—personified in the character Pedro Barrera—who refuse to forget the Civil War and old hostilities. The problem presented in the comedy was a significant one for Spain in the period; but the solution presented by Ruiz Iriarte is merely a stock literary device.

Springtime in the Plaza de París has two acts, each of which is divided into two scenes. As the action begins several hours have passed since the curtain fell on *The Girl in the Little Pink Hat*. The initial scene, which takes place in the late evening, is largely exposition for the benefit of those who did not see the first play. Although it is clear that Leonor still loves Esteban, she assigns him sleeping quarters at the other end of the apartment from her own room. The second scene, which introduces the principal dramatic situation of the comedy, begins the following morning with the arrival of Pedro

Barrera. Although he and Esteban despite their differing political viewpoints were friends before the war, the conservative Pedro considers Esteban and all other liberals to be his mortal enemies. He is appalled to learn that the rumors he has heard about Leonor's acceptance of Esteban and his daughters into her home are true. Esteban finds that he is under attack not only from Pedro and the extreme right, but also from the old left. He has begun to receive anonymous letters telling him that his return to Spain was a betrayal of their cause.

It is obviously Ruiz Iriarte's intention to satirize the older generation and its unwillingness to forget the Civil War. The hope for the future lies with a new generation that rejects bitterness and hatred. The younger generation is personified in Perico, Pedro's idealistic, liberal son who greatly admires Esteban and his writings, even if the older man from the perspective of the young is reactionary. Leonor quickly perceives the possibility of bringing Esteban and Pedro together through their children. Perico and Marita obligingly fall in love. When the two fathers oppose the weddings, Leonor helps the young people run away and spend the night together so that the fathers' Spanish code of honor will require them to marry. The Romeo and Juliet story has a happy ending, with the reconciliation not only of the two men but also of Esteban and Leonor as husband and wife.

Springtime in the Plaza de París shared the success of *The Girl in the Little Pink Hat* although in several respects it is less profound and convincing. The characters of the sequel play lack the psychological depth of the portrayal of, in particular, Leonor in the first comedy. Pedro and Perico, who share the spotlight with Leonor, are stereotypes representing the immovable older conservative and the idealistic young liberal. As Perico tells his father, ". . . you believe in the past and I believe in the future. . . . I protest and you conform." [11] On the one hand, Perico and Marita represent a new generation, but on the other hand they rather unbelievably follow the same code of conduct their elders accept. To a large extent, *Springtime in the Plaza de París* is more farcical than *The Girl in the Little Pink Hat* both in terms of characterization and plot development.

At the level of farce, Ruiz Iriarte constructs the comedy with his usual skill. He builds the action revolving around Perico and Marita on a series of comic reversals. For example, Leonor is at first unconcerned that Marita has run off with Perico, for she herself has engineered the episode and sent Damián along as a chaperone. When

Esteban wants to call the Civil Guard, she scoffs. But when Damián returns alone, indicating that Perico and Marita did indeed spend the night together, it is Leonor who wants to contact the police. A second comic reversal takes place with the arrival of the two young people and Marita's explanation that Perico left her alone in a hotel. Undoubtedly the audience as well as the older characters heaved a sigh of relief.

The action of the comedy takes place in autumn, but it is springtime in the Plaza de París anyway, springtime representing love and hope. The ending is, as one critic noted at the time, evocative of Benavente.[12] In providing the reconciliation among his characters, Ruiz Iriarte hopes to encourage a softened political attitude on the part of at least some of the audience as well. Pedro in the final scenes admits that the old guard he represents no longer has much influence: "Those who command now are the liberals, the progressives, the technocrats" (*SP*, 80). If this appraisal was not totally true in 1968, it certainly was validated by the election results in Spain in 1977. Pedro feels that he has been defeated by the others; but he is also relieved at the outcome of the conflict. "Hatred and rancor weigh heavily . . . . And now I realize, although I did not dare say it to myself, that this is what I've always hoped for, this is what I've always wanted with all my heart. To forget. And to begin again. To live!" (*SP*, 84). The final message of the play, one of which Leonor in her wisdom and understanding of human nature was aware before either Pedro or Esteban, is that life is far too short to waste time and energy on hostility, and that love is far more important to happiness than ideology. Unquestionably *Springtime in the Plaza de París* represents the epitome of Ruiz Iriarte's optimism.

IV Good Evening, Sabina

Buenas noches, Sabina [Good Evening, Sabina] opened in the Arlequín theater of Madrid on September 25, 1975, and was directed by the playwright himself.[13] As is usually the case with comedies by Ruiz Iriarte, the play has been praised for its "ingenious dialogue" and its "technical know-how."[14] One reviewer observed that it is a rare example of a "classic comedy," noteworthy for its dialogue, its psychological development of character, its irony, intelligence and sentiment.[15] Consisting of two acts, divided into five scenes, preceded by a prologue, the comedy has only one stage setting, the well furnished apartment of Sabina and Manuel. Manuel is an intellectual professor, a character somewhat reminiscent of the male protagonists of *The Poor Little Liar* or *The Girl in the Little Pink Hat*. Sabina is his proper Spanish wife. As one critic has noted, both of them have something in common with the *pobrecito* characters of the earlier comedies.[16] But unlike the comedies of the 1950s, in this play both husband and wife are capable of commiting adultery.

The prologue, which takes place while the stage is in darkness, consists of the voices of Sabina and Nicolás, an attractive man she meets at a party. As the play itself begins, Sabina has arrived home and calls her friend Amparo to confess that she has been seduced by Nicolás. Amparo, Sabina's lifelong friend who has remained unmarried, is worldly-wise and stands in vivid contrast to the traditional wife who is mortified by her sinful adventure. Sabina's sense of remorse is enhanced by her conviction that Manuel is a saint. In the early part of the play, Ruiz Iriarte exploits the irony in Manuel's belief that his wife is virtuous and incapable of any wrong-doing. Eventually, however, we learn that Amparo is Manuel's mistress. From that point on the comedy is structured on a double irony, for neither spouse is aware of the other's infidelity. In the kind of reversal of values that appeared with some frequency in the comedies of manners, Sabina wishes that Manuel were unfaithful to her. Her assumption is that if he were a scoundrel rather than a perfect husband, he would be more likely to forgive her for her momentary lapse.

In *When She Is the Other Woman*, Ruiz Iriarte developed his plot around two couples, saving the marriage of the husband and wife when his mistress and her admirer go off together. The solution in *Good Evening, Sabina* is very similar. At the conclusion Nicolás takes Amparo with him to Stockholm. Manuel and Sabina confess their guilt to one another and in a scene of reconciliation, reminiscent of Benavente, determine that they can forgive and forget. Manuel, who is basically a *pobrecito*, has lost loves to this same Nicolás before. He and Sabina both realize that for them the permanency of marriage, even though it may upon occasion lack romance and excitement, is of far more importance than brief interludes with other partners. Adolfo Prego, who was critical of the change in tone which takes place in the middle of the play, summarized the moral of the story as follows: "There is a way of life where happiness is peaceful, orderly and, in a certain way, boring, and from which one should not stray because the other kind of happiness, that which startles with its maximum intensity and its passionate extravagance, ends disastrously." [17]

Unlike the female characters in such comedies of manners as

Child's Play and *When She Is the Other Woman*, Sabina actually does commit adultery, but in most respects she is very similar to the Spanish wives in the earlier plays and Ruiz Iriarte maintains his attitude in support of traditional values and institutions. Because she is unaware of his guilt Sabina does not set out to make a philandering husband jealous. Her infidelity is attributable to her overindulgence in alcoholic beverages, the seductive appeal of Nicolás, and a fleeting desire to escape from the humdrum quality of her daily life. Her feeling of remorse, however, outweighs her pleasure—in which sense, like the traditional women in the plays of the 1950s, she is unable to set aside her ingrained concept of right and wrong. In the final scene of reconciliation, Ruiz Iriarte reinforces the view that happiness lies in the acceptance of traditional moral values, not in sexual liberation. The comedy unquestionably would appeal to an older middle-class audience; Francisco Álvaro points out that its success may be attributable to the fact that Ruiz Iriarte, although he has staged few new plays in recent years, has a large and loyal following.[18]

CHAPTER 9

Conclusion

JOHN Dowling, in his recent study of the comic theater of the postwar period in Spain, has observed not only that comedy has predominated over other forms of theater but also that Spanish literature in general tends to have a moral, didactic point of view.[1] Spanish theater, which has seldom accepted a rigorous division between comedy and tragedy, rather has required comic relief in serious drama and a serious content in light comedy. "The writer of comedies who combines utility with pleasure is writing for an audience that delights in mixing laughter and tears."[2] Dowling further notes that in the contemporary period, no one has understood this lesson better than Víctor Ruiz Iriarte. In the thirty-five years of his writing career, Ruiz Iriarte has turned his talents to various genres and media, including newspaper essays, film scripts, and television plays, and has created stage plays ranging from farce to serious drama. He has, however, remained primarily a writer of comedies and as such has captured well the mood of his public. His comic theater may on occasion develop a theme of poetic fantasy or consist merely of a game without transcendental intent, but usually, as Dowling correctly affirms, Ruiz Iriarte's comic theater has been oriented to giving a "commentary on the human condition" and, by showing the foibles of society and human nature, to educating his audience.[3]

Because his underlying purpose is often serious, sometimes Ruiz Iriarte's comedies seem to shift direction from their first act to the second. The beginning is presented in the tone and rhythm of light comedy or farce while the conclusion takes a turn toward the moral or sentimental. Critics have found this tendency to be a significant weakness in some of his plays.[4] At his best, Ruiz Iriarte blends the tragic and the comic throughout his work, allowing the serious implications to hover beneath the superficial level of light comedy. There is no question that the major plays are well written and entertaining. Less obvious but equally true is that they contain a critical testimony of the changes in postwar Spanish society, particularly of the upper middle-class.

Ruiz Iriarte's satire, while usually gentle in tone, nevertheless makes fun of many aspects of contemporary Spanish life: the decay in the traditional family structure, the disappearance of strong religious and moral values, the overemphasis on material possessions and social status, the generation gap, the influence of foreign cultures on Spanish ways of life. As a vehicle for depicting society as he sees it, Ruiz Iriarte introduces several series of repeated characters. His *pobrecito*, an antihero in the early comedies, reflects the inverted values of today's world; although a virtuous person, he is considered a failure by those who reject inner worth in favor of superficial glamour. In the later plays, Ruiz Iriarte reveals a hidden truth about those who are admired by society for their material success. At heart they are as isolated and perhaps even more unhappy than the *pobrecito* characters and are just as incapable of escaping from their roles in life. Across the years, Ruiz Iriarte develops an interesting spectrum of female characters, some of whom share the characteristics of the *pobrecito*, some of whom represent the worst aspects of a frivolous, materialistic society, but others of whom incarnate the strength of character and the love for other human beings that Ruiz Iriarte apparently sees as the necessary requisites for achieving true happiness on either the individual or collective scales.

From his childhood on, Ruiz Iriarte has loved theater. He has expressed this love not only in his essays but in his dedication to his profession. For him there is an overlap between theater and life, and he has accordingly shown an interest in the works of other playwrights, such as Pirandello, Evreinov, and Anouilh, who have also understood the interrelationship of fiction and reality. Among the best of his early works are plays of poetic fantasy in which his characters escape from their harsh existences through a kind of theatricalized life. In many of his plays, including the more realistic comedies of manners and some of his later works, Ruiz Iriarte introduces characters who deliberately assume roles for themselves, or dreamers who may find happiness in imaginary loves. Even without this kind of play-within-a-play, there is found frequently in his works the suggestion that life itself is theater—perhaps tragedy, perhaps vaudeville, but more likely tragicomedy—that same blend of humor and pathos which underlies most of his own plays.

A polished craftsman, Ruiz Iriarte has excelled most consistently in his careful play construction and in his sparkling dialogue. Quite possibly in these respects, as well as in his choice of themes he has established himself as a model to other Spanish playwrights.[5] Unquestionably, he has created works that have met with commercial success. While some critics have rejected Ruiz Iriarte's kind of theater because it evades the most pressing economic and social problems of contemporary Spain, by its very nature it is less limited in its potential appeal to audiences than social realism, and his plays continue to be staged both in Spain and in other countries. In 1969, for example, the year in which *Story of Adultery* premièred in Madrid, *The Six-Horse Landau* (1950) was staged in England; *The Poor Little Liar* (1953), in Argentina; *Tonight Is the Prelude* (1958), in Portugal; *I Have a Million* (1960), in Argentina and Portugal; and *The Carousel* (1964), in Belgium.[6]

Ruiz Iriarte has himself observed that theater is ephemeral; plays are written in the language and spirit of a given moment to quickly become dated. Nevertheless it is likely that some of his own plays will prove to be of lasting interest. Among those that promise to endure are *The Six-Horse Landau, The Grand Minuet, The Carousel,* and *Story of Adultery.* Ruiz Iriarte is conscious of the theatricality required of a staged play, and his staging techniques have evolved and developed over the years. In his most important works, he combines this theatricality with themes and characters that reflect the human condition, while imbuing his vision of society with poetry and humor. He is at all times a spectator, one who, standing off to the side may see life metaphorically as a game, a ball, a merry-go-round, but whose satire and occasional scepticism are tempered always with a genuine sympathy for the characters he portrays. His collective works, including the ones that have been labeled escapist, stand as a document that directly and indirectly reflects the reality of the Spanish middle-class and the changing values of postwar Spain. As such, they will continue to be of literary and sociological interest long after their days on the boards.

Notes and References

Chapter One

1. I am indebted to Ruiz Iriarte for his cooperation in supplying biographical data in our interview of June 22, 1977, and in a personal letter dated November 2, 1977. The principal source of information on his childhood and early career is his four-part memoirs "Viaje alrededor de un escenario" published in the journal *Teatro*: 1 (November, 1952), 41-45; 2 (December, 1952), 42-47; 3 (January, 1953), 37-41; 6 (April, 1953), 25-30. References to the memoirs are cited in the text as *T* with volume and page numbers. Unless otherwise indicated, all translations into English are my own.

2. The most extensive development of the subject is found in his *Tres maestros (Arniches, Benavente y Valle-Inclán)* (Madrid: Real Escuela Superior de Arte Dramático, 1965).

3. "Prólogo" to *Tres comedias optimistas* (Madrid: 1947), p. 5.

4. *Ibid.*, p. 6.

5. *Teatro* 3: 41. In these memoirs, Ruiz Iriarte never mentions that his short stature undoubtedly made his situation as an unknown writer more difficult than that of his struggling contemporaries. Under four and a half feet tall, he perhaps was given even less serious consideration as a playwright than others of his age and experience. It is perhaps also because of his physical condition that he tends in his theater to portray with sympathy a series of characters, both male and female, who do not fit society's stereotyped ideal images and suggests, instead, that we should look for the real person under the superficial appearance.

6. Domingo Orta, "Gente de teatro en España (I): Víctor Ruiz Iriarte," *Teatro* 17 (September-December, 1955), p. 32. Other quotations in this paragraph are from the same source.

7. Orta, p. 31.

8. Julio Trenas, "Víctor Ruiz Iriarte, Presidente de la S.G.A.E.," *ABC*, July 22, 1969, unpaged.

9. Holt, *The Contemporary Spanish Theater (1949-1972)* (Boston: Twayne, 1975), p. 31.

10. Lorenzo López Sancho, "Prólogo" to Esteban Lendínez-Gallego, *El teatro de Ruiz Iriarte* (Madrid: Ediciones Cultura Hispánica, 1973), p. 10.

11. Arcadio Baquero Goyanes, "El humor en el teatro de Ruiz Iriarte," in J. Rof Carballo *et al*, *El teatro de humor en España* (Madrid: Editora Nacional, 1966), p. 197.

12. *Ibid.*

13.   J. Rodríguez Richart, "Entre renovación y tradición. Direcciones principales del teatro español actual," *Boletín Bibliográfico de Menéndez Pelayo* 41 (1965), 397.

14.   Ignacio Soldevilla Durante, "Sobre el teatro español de los últimos 25 años," *Cuadernos Americanos*, 126 (1963), 279.

15.   Enrique Sordo, "El teatro español desde 1936 hasta 1966" in *Historia general de las literaturas hispánicas*, Vol. VI, ed. Guillermo Díaz Plaja (Barcelona: Vergara, 1967), p. 778.

16.   José Monleón, *Treinta años de teatro de la derecha* (Barcelona: Tusquets, 1971), p. 82.

17.   Monleón, p. 13.

18.   Monleón, p. 82.

19.   Hartnoll, *A Concise History of the Theater* (New York: Charles Scribner's Sons, no date), p. 214.

20.   Rodríguez Richart, p. 398.

21.   Domingo Pérez Minik, "Tres curanderos de la realidad," in *Teatro europeo contemporáneo* (Madrid: Guadarrama, 1961), pp. 453-55.

22.   Article from *La Estafeta Literaria* quoted by Baquero Goyanes, p. 187.

23.   "Prólogo" to *Tres comedias optimistas*, p. 5.

24.   Baquero Goyanes, p. 198.

25.   Personal interview, June 22, 1977.

26.   John Dowling in his recent study "Teatro cómico y lo cómico en el teatro español de la posguerra" notes both that comedies predominate in the Sainz de Robles anthologies from 1949 to 1973 and that Ruiz Iriarte is the writer of comedies most frequently represented. [*Hispania*, 60 (1977), 901]

27.   In his interview with Orta, Ruiz Iriarte specifically mentions favorable criticism of his plays from London and Brazil and notes that *El landó de seis caballos* was well received in Philadelphia and Holland (pp. 76-77). As mentioned earlier, many of his plays have been staged in other Spanish-speaking countries. The playwright also refers to German translations of works by López Rubio, Alfonso Paso and himself in his "Alfonso Paso," *Primer Acto*, 3 (Summer, 1957), 21.

28.   Aurelio Labajo, Carlos Urdiales, Trini González, eds., *El teatro de 1950*, Vol. I (Madrid: Coculsa, 1970), p. 23.

Chapter Two

1.   Personal interview, June 22, 1977.

2.   Ruiz Iriarte destroyed all of his earlier plays. See his prologue to *Tres comedias optimistas*, p. 3.

3.   Isabel Magaña Schevill, "Introduction" to *Juego de niños* (Englewood Cliffs, N. J.: Prentice-Hall, 1965), n. 1, p. ix.

4.   See Sordo, p. 778, and Rodríguez Richart, *Vida y teatro de Alejandro Casona* (Oviedo: Instituto de Estudios Asturianos, 1963), pp. 73-74. The latter criticism of *El puente de los suicidas* is extremely negative.

5. Ángel Valbuena Prat, *Historia del teatro español* (Barcelona: Noguer, 1956), pp. 654, 666.

6. Very few critics have noted the influence of Evreinov on either Ruiz Iriarte or Casona. See, however, Alfredo Marqueríe, "Víctor Ruiz Iriarte o la sonrisa," in *El teatro: Enciclopedia del arte escénica*, ed. Guillermo Díaz Plaja (Barcelona: Noguer, 1958), p. 500; review of *Los árboles mueren de pie*, *La Nación*, Buenos Aires, April 2, 1949, quoted by Rodríguez Richart, "Casona en Norteamérica," *Boletín del Instituto de Estudios Asturianos*, 20, lvii (April, 1966), 7. The latter critic links both Casona and Ruiz Iriarte with Evreinov. See also my "Casona and Evreinov: Life as Theater," *Modern Drama*, 22 (1979), 77-88.

7. Christopher Collins, "Nikolai Evreinov as a Playwright" in *Life As Theater: Five Modern Plays by Nikolai Evreinov*, trans. Collins (Ann Arbor, Mich.: Ardis, 1973), p. xxvii.

8. George Kalbouss, "The Plays of Nikolai Evreinov," *Russian Language Journal*, 92 (1971), 31.

9. Casona, *La sirena varada* (Madrid: Espasa-Calpe, 1977), pp. 15-16.

10. Kessel Schwartz, "Reality in the Works of Alejandro Casona," *Hispania*, 40 (1957), 60.

11. Sainz de Robles, "Prólogo" to *Alejandro Casona, Obras completas*, Vol. I (Madrid: Aguilar, 1966), p. cxxxv.

12. *Academia de amor* in *Tres comedias optimistas*, pp. 132-33. References are to this edition and are cited in the text as *A*.

13. See, for example, Charles H. Leighton, "Alejandro Casona's 'Pirandellism,' " *Symposium*, 17 iii (1963), 202-14; Peter Standish, "Pirandello, Pygmalion, and Spain," *Revue de Littérature Comparée*, 47 (1973), 327-37; Wilma Newberry, *The Pirandellian Mode in Spanish Literature from Cervantes to Sastre* (Albany, N.Y.: State Univ. of New York Press, 1973). Newberry's book, which includes a number of articles previously published in various journals, mentions a dozen twentieth-century Spanish playwrights but omits Ruiz Iriarte. Valbuena Prat does link *El puente de los suicidas* with Casona's Pirandellism (*Historia del teatro español*, p. 654), and the relationship between *El landó de seis caballos* and Pirandello's *Enrico IV* has been mentioned with some frequency. See Holt, pp. 99-100, and my "Fantasy and Lunacy in the Contemporary Spanish Theatre," *Kentucky Foreign Language Quarterly*, Supplement 13 (1967), 41-51. See also my "The Pirandellism of Víctor Ruiz Iriarte," *Estreno* 4 ii (Fall, 1978), 18-21.

14. I am in general agreement with Leighton that Casona does not share Pirandello's basic philosophy. See "Alejandro Casona y las ideas," *Insula*, 206 (1964), 15. Ruiz Iriarte, at least in his early plays, and Casona also both differ from Pirandello and Evreinov in that they make no similar systematic effort to destroy the illusionism of the stage.

15. *El puente de los suicidas* in *Tres comedias optimistas*, p. 76.

16. Lendínez-Gallego identifies loneliness, love, and the family as Ruiz Iriarte's dominant theme. See *El teatro de Ruiz Iriarte*, pp. 99-128.

17. Baquero Goyanes, pp. 189-96. Because no English term adequately

renders the sense of "pobre hombre" or "pobrecito," I shall in the text use the Spanish *pobrecito*. The feminine form, referring to a woman who is not attractive to men and therefore goes unnoticed, is *pobrecita*.

18.   Schevill, p. xviii. Her analysis does not include *Academia de amor*, but the device she identifies in the plays beginning with *El aprendiz de amante* is present here as well.

19.   Holt, p. 98.

20.   Gerald E. Wade, "The Comedies of Victor Ruiz Iriarte," *Hispania*, 45 (1962), 707.

21.   Marquerie, review reprinted in *Teatro español 1949-1950*, ed. Sainz de Robles (Madrid: Aguilar, 1951), p. 308.

22.   Schevill, xviii.

23.   A complete list of Spanish plays related thematically to *El landó de seis caballos* would be very long indeed. The interested reader is referred to María Victoria Morales, "The Farcical Mode in the Spanish Theater of the Twentieth Century" (Ph.D. dissertation, Columbia University, 1969) and my "The Bases of Humor in the Contemporary Spanish Theater" (Ph.D. dissertation, University of Florida, 1965).

24.   Holt, p. 99.

25.   Holt, p. 100.

26.   Marquerie discusses this aspect of the play in his review, p. 309.

27.   Holt says that *El landó de seis caballos* "lies somewhere between certain plays of Marcel Achard and those of Jean Anouilh in its Pirandellian inspiration" (p. 99).

28.   Morales suggests that the four have been chosen "among those living in loneliness and despair" (p. 260).

29.   *El landó de seis caballos* in *Teatro selecto de Víctor Ruiz Iriarte* (Madrid: Escelicer, 1967), p. 52.

30.   Schevill identifies *El café de las flores* as having the same basic dramatic formula as *La soltera rebelde*, *El pobrecito embustero*, *El aprendiz de amante*, *Las mujeres decentes*, and *Juego de niños*, all plays which I analyze in Chapter 4.

31.   The reviewer for *Teatro* considered this opening the best first act Ruiz Iriarte had written [9 (September-December, 1953), p. 5].

32.   *El café de las flores* (Madrid: Alfil, 1953), p. 46. References are to this edition and are cited in the text as *C*.

33.   Valbuena Prat, p. 665.

Chapter Three

1.   Alfredo Marquerie, *Veinte años de teatro en España* (Madrid: Editora Nacional, 1959), p. 169.

2.   Pérez Minik, p. 459.

3.   Ruiz Iriarte himself identifies four plays as satires, including *El pobrecito embustero* in the group. [See Orta, p. 32.] I have chosen to discuss

this work with the comedies of manners because of the similarity in its dramatic formula.

4. José Gordon selected *Un día en la gloria* for inclusion in his *Teatro experimental español (Antología e historia)* (Madrid: Escelicer, 1965). Conceivably some of the early plays Ruiz Iriarte chose to destroy were written in this same vein.

5. *Un día en la gloria* (Madrid: Alfil, 1952), p. 75. References are to this edition and cited in the text as *D*.

6. Marqueríe identifies an influence of George Bernard Shaw in this play (*Veinte años*, p. 169) as does Lendínez-Gallego (p. 35). I am at a loss to explain why. Shaw did delight in debunking myths and he did deal with Joan of Arc, Napoleon, and Don Juan in separate plays, but his works are not so fanciful as *A Day in Glory* and I find it doubtful that there is a direct influence of Shaw here.

7. Wade, p. 705.

8. *El gran minué* in *Teatro selecto*, pp. 101-02. References are to this edition and are cited in the text as *G*.

9. Holt, p. 101.

10. A Giraudoux kind of humor may be found in several other Spanish plays besides *El gran minué*. See my "Traces of Giraudoux in the Contemporary Spanish Theatre," *Romance Notes*, 11 (1969), 8-11.

11. Ruiz Iriarte, "Prólogo" to *Teatro selecto*, p. 7.

12. Díez Crespo in his review of the play calls it "la farsa y licencia de un rey," an allusion to Valle-Inclán's satirical attack on Isabel II (reprinted in *Teatro español 1950-1951*, ed. Sainz de Robles. Madrid: Aguilar, 1952, p. 166). I find the comparison of doubtful validity.

13. Holt, pp. 101-02. Holt's comment was made in response to Wade's suggestion that *The Grand Minuet* is a morality play in reverse with Ruiz Iriarte "nodding approval" at immorality (pp. 705-06). I believe that Wade has missed the point of Ruiz Iriarte's satire.

14. I disagree with Angel Zuñiga who called this a "typical play" by Ruiz Iriarte (review reprinted in *Teatro español 1950-1951*, p. 168).

15. I also disagree with Luis Molero Manglano who suggests that Ruiz Iriarte tends to evoke "la belle époque" and cites *El landó de seis caballos*, *La cena de los Reyes Magos* [sic], *Un paraguas bajo la lluvia*, *Cuando la guerra de Cuba* [sic], *El gran minué*" as evidence of this tendency ("El teatro de Ruiz Iriarte" in *Teatro español contemporáneo*. Madrid: Editora Nacional, 1974, pp. 175-76.) *La cena de los tres reyes* has a contemporary setting, as does *El landó de seis caballos* except for the recreation of the past by the old people. As we shall see in a later chapter, *Un paraguas bajo la lluvia* takes place only partially in the past. That leaves *El gran minué* and *La guerra empieza en Cuba* as the only plays with historical settings.

16. Marqueríe, *Veinte años*, p. 174.

17. *La cena de los tres reyes* (Madrid: Alfil, 1955), pp. 96-97. References are to this edition and are cited in the text as *K*.

18. Schevill, p. xx.
19. Gonzalo Torrente Ballester, *Teatro español contemporáneo*. 2nd ed. (Madrid: Guadarrama, 1968), p. 585.

Chapter Four

1. Valbuena Prat, p. 665.
2. Valbuena Prat, p. 670.
3. Schevill, ix-xviii. Subsequent references to Schevill in the following section are to those pages. As noted in Chapter 2, I have chosen to place *El café de las flores* with the plays of poetic fantasy rather than here with the comedies of manners.
4. The male critics, writing in the early 1960s, apparently accepted the aggressive Don Juan and the shy female as normal sex roles and therefore did not identify the *pobrecita* counterpart to the *pobrecito*.
5. Pérez Minik, p. 458. Neither this critic nor those who later accepted his observation identify the *pobrecitos* in Cervantes, Galdós or Arniches to which he refers. The obvious Cervantine example is Alonso Quijano in *Don Quixote*. In Galdós the most developed character of this type is Maxi in *Fortunata y Jacinta*. In Arniches, the *pobrecito* is almost a stock type and may be found in such plays as *Es mi hombre* and *El señor Badanas*. Critics often mention an influence of Arniches on Ruiz Iriarte. One area where this is obviously apparent is in the repeated use of the *pobrecito*.
6. Baquero Goyanes, pp. 189-96.
7. Orta, p. 32.
8. Pérez Minik, pp. 458-59.
9. Molero Manglano, p. 175.
10. López Sancho, p. 14.
11. Trenas.
12. Personal interview, June 22, 1977.
13. *El aprendiz de amante*. (Madrid: Alfil, 1952), p. 18. References are to this edition and are cited in the text as *AL*.
14. Schevill, p. xii.
15. Pérez Minik, p. 459.
16. See, for example, Marquerie, "Víctor Ruiz Iriarte o la sonrisa," p. 500 and Pérez Minik, p. 460.
17. Curiously, Wade in his study of Ruiz Iriarte's comedies says that Spanish comedy in the period was "clear and clean" and that "no Spanish playwright has yet found the gold in the golden-hearted prostitute" (pp. 708-09). He has apparently overlooked Paulina, Manolita, and several other characters in Ruiz Iriarte's comedies along with a number of Miguel Mihura's heroines. McKay finds that "happy hookers" appear in six of Mihura's twenty-two published plays. See Douglas R. McKay, *Miguel Mihura* (Boston: Twayne, 1977), pp. 116–17.
18. Schevill, p. xvi.

19. Schevill, p. xvi; Morales, p. 109.

20. *Las mujeres decentes*, published with *El gran minué* (Madrid: Alfil, 1951), p. 88.

21. In *Un pequeño mundo* (Madrid: 1962), pp. 59-62.

22. Torrente Ballester notes a parallel between *Cuando ella es la otra* and one of Benavente's last comedies but explains that the situation was "in the air" at the time (p. 583). The contrast between the proper Spanish girl and an emancipated American forms the basis of Luca de Tena and Miguel de la Cuesta's *Dos mujeres a las nueve* (1949). The contrast between two Spanish women is seen in López Rubio's *Diana está comunicando* (1960). The traditional Spanish woman was caricatured as early as Mihura's *Tres sombreros de copa* (written in 1932, staged in 1952) in the person of Dionisio's fiancée who never appears on stage; the changing role of women in society goes back even further, forming part of the basis of Benavente's *Lo cursi* (1901). The examples of contrasts between emancipated younger women and traditional older women are numerous and include some of Ruiz Iriarte's comedies discussed later in this chapter.

23. Entrambasaguas, *El año literario (1952)* (Madrid: Consejo Superior de Investigaciones Científicas, 1953), p. 13; Torrente Ballester, p. 583. Torrente believes that the plot, being very thin, does not justify a three-act play.

24. Baquero Goyanes, pp. 192-93.

25. *Cuando ella es la otra* (Madrid: Alfil, 1952), p. 29.

26. Valbuena Prat, p. 670.

27. Holt translates *Juego de niños* as *A Dangerous Game* (p. 102), but I prefer the more literal, and hence more ironic, title.

28. See *Teatro* 13 (October-December, 1954), 38-39.

29. Fernando Méndez-Leite, *Historia del cine español*, Vol. II (Madrid: Rialp, 1965), p. 342.

30. See Sainz de Robles, *Teatro español 1951-1952* (Madrid: Aguilar, 1953), p. 12; and Antonio Abad Ojuel in *Teatro español 1951-1952*, p. 226.

31. Baquero Goyanes, p. 194.

32. *Juego de niños*. 4th ed. (Madrid: Alfil, 1965), p. 58. References are to this edition and are cited in the text as *J*.

33. Ruiz Iriarte, "Autocrítica" in *Teatro español, 1951-1952*, p. 223.

34. Torrente Ballester, pp. 579-80. Torrente's criticism of the play is generally negative.

35. Schevill, p. x.

36. Torrente Ballester, p. 581.

37. Ruiz Iriarte, in our interview of June 22, 1977, indicated that he did write some of his plays with certain actors in mind, notably Tina Gascó, Carmen Carbonell, Antonio Vico, Enrique Diosdado, and Amelia de la Torre. He does not believe that the practice affected his creative freedom.

38. Obviously Lupe's advice is more in keeping with traditional views of women's role in society than with contemporary feminist thought.

39.   Wade, p. 707.
40.   Ruiz Iriarte himself classifies *El pobrecito embustero* as a satirical comedy, not a comedy of manners. See Orta, p. 32.
41.   *El aprendiz de amante* was staged in Madrid in the season preceding Sainz de Robles' publication of his yearly anthology and hence would not have been considered.
42.   Holt, p. 102.
43.   Carlos Fernández Cuenca, "Un mes de teatro en Madrid," *Teatro* 7 (May, 1953), 5.
44.   A. Rodríguez de León, review reprinted in *Teatro español, 1952-1953*, ed. Sainz de Robles (Madrid: Aguilar, 1954), p. 300. It is a critical commonplace to say that Ruiz Iriarte is influenced by Roussin. Although there is generally little in common between the two playwrights, Rodríguez de León is the only critic I have found who rejects the comparison.
45.   Baquero Goyanes, p. 198.
46.   *El pobrecito embustero*, in *Teatro español, 1952-1953*, p. 352. References are to this edition and are cited in the text as *P*.
47.   Torrente Ballester, p. 584.
48.   Torrente Ballester, p. 586.
49.   Wade, p. 707; Pérez Minik, p. 460.

Chapter Five

1.   Personal interview, June 22, 1977.
2.   Ruiz Iriarte, "Prólogo" to *Teatro selecto*, p. 11.
3.   J. Téllez Moreno, review reprinted in *Teatro español, 1965-1966*, ed. Sainz de Robles (Madrid: Aguilar, 1967), p. 102.
4.   This is the term (*juego teatral*) Ruiz Iriarte uses to describe *La guerra empieza en Cuba* (Orta, p. 32). He defines *Un paraguas bajo la lluvia* with the related French expression *jeu d'esprit* ("Prólogo" to *Teatro selecto*, p. 11).
5.   Trenas.
6.   Ruiz Iriarte, "Autocrítica" in *Teatro español, 1955-1956*, ed. Sainz de Robles (Madrid: Aguilar, 1957), p. 3.
7.   Torrente Ballester, p. 587. Shakespeare also introduced a second set of twins in *The Comedy of Errors*.
8.   Luis Marsillach, review reprinted in *Teatro español, 1955-1956*, p. 6.
9.   Méndez-Leite, p. 290.
10.   The term "well-made play" originally was used to describe the works of Eugène Scribe and his followers in the early nineteenth century and obviously connotes careful construction for construction's sake. I am not in agreement with Wade, who apparently overlooked the careful construction of *La guerra empieza en Cuba* when he stated that "the plot becomes so confused that the author fails to manipulate it efficiently" (Wade, p. 706).
11.   The second act here is long enough to be two acts. All of Ruiz Iriarte's full-length plays prior to *La guerra empieza en Cuba* except *El landó de seis*

caballos were divided into three acts. Subsequent plays, consistent with the recent practice in the Spanish theater, are two-act plays. Typically there are two performances of plays daily, an afternoon presentation at 7:00, ending before the Spanish supper hour, and an after-supper night performance starting between 10:30 and 11:00. To remain within the rigid time constraints imposed by this format, playwrights generally limit themselves to two acts with one intermission.

12.   In this analysis I am following to some extent the principles outlined by Paul M. Levitt in his *A Structural Approach to the Analysis of Drama* (The Hague: Mouton, 1971).

13.   Among the many plays that use ghosts for comic effect are Jardiel Poncela's *Un marido de ida y vuelta* (1939), Noel Coward's *Blithe Spirit* (1941) and Soriano de Andia's *Ayer . . . será mañana* (1951). The device itself is clearly no more original with Ruiz Iriarte than were the twins in *La guerra empieza en Cuba*. Usually the principal comic effect achieved with the ghost occurs by having the figure visible and audible only to some of the characters, not to others. Ruiz Iriarte uses the figure this way only in the final scene when Mateo finds Florita talking to her departed mother and is distressed to learn that he will have a ghost for a mother-in-law. Throughout the mother-daughter dialogues, however, Ruiz Iriarte plays with the ideas that Doña Florita is dead, that she did not go to heaven, etc.

14.   José Montero Alonso, review reprinted in *Teatro español, 1965-1966*, p. 103.

15.   Ruiz Iriarte, "Prólogo" to *Teatro selecto*, p. 11.

16.   See Holt, pp. 31-32. Some of the moral taboos that persisted after 1963 disappeared during the 1975-76 theatrical season when partial nudity was allowed on the Spanish stage for the first time and sexual themes became quite bold.

Chapter Six

1.   Marqueríe's phrase, "un comediógrafo que iba para dramaturgo" appears both in "Víctor Ruiz Iriarte o la sonrisa," p. 499, and *Veinte años de teatro en España*, pp. 167, 169. In his article "Nuestros autores de postguerra" he predicts that someday Ruiz Iriarte will return to "the major key" for which he has unquestionable talent. See *Teatro*, 19 (May-August, 1956), 12.

2.   Personal interview, June 22, 1977.

3.   Holt, p. 109.

4.   Trenas.

5.   Lendínez-Gallego, p. 133.

6.   Schevill, p. xxi. Marqueríe categorizes *Los pájaros ciegos* as naked drama and *Esta noche es la víspera* as one of Ruiz Iriarte's three outstanding plays (*Veinte años de teatro en España*, pp. 169, 176).

7.   As indicated earlier, I am limiting my discussion to the published plays.

8.   Molero Manglano, pp. 177-83.

9. *Juanita va a Rio de Janeiro* in *Colección Teatro (Extra)*, No. 100 (Madrid: Alfil, 1954), p. 148.

10. See Ruiz Iriarte's "Autocrítica" to *Esta noche es la víspera* in *Teatro español, 1958-1959* (Madrid: Aguilar, 1960), p. 125, and the "Prólogo" to his *Teatro selecto*, pp. 7-8.

11. Schevill, p. xxi; Holt, p. 104; Merrill, "Introduction" to *Esta noche es la víspera* (Indianapolis and New York: Odyssey, 1968), p. vii.

12. Review from *Arriba* quoted in Francisco Álvaro, *El espectador y la crítica: El teatro en España en 1958* (Valladolid and Madrid: Sever-Cuesta, 1959), p. 110.

13. Holt, p. 104.

14. *Esta noche es la víspera* in *Teatro selecto*, p. 247. References are to this edition and are cited in the text as *N*.

15. "Autocrítica," p. 126.

16. Marqueríe makes this observation and cites a recent play of Alfonso Paso in his review, reprinted in *Teatro español, 1958-1959*, p. 127. Sainz de Robles specifically mentions Casona's *Siete gritos en el mar (Teatro español, 1958-1959*, p. xx). In spite of the long tradition of this kind of play featuring a group of characters, Wade curiously labeled *Tonight Is the Prelude* as "technically imperfect" because "we cannot decide who the protagonist really is" (p. 706).

17. *Dear Antoine*, trans. Lucienne Hill (London: Methuen, 1971), p. 20.

18. Marqueríe review reprinted in *Teatro español, 1958-1959*, p. 127.

19. See my "Macabre Humor in the Contemporary Spanish Theater," *Romance Notes*, 9 (1968), 201-05.

20. Sainz de Robles called this play an "ingenious caricature of a detective drama." See *Teatro español, 1957-1958* (Madrid: Aguilar, 1959), p. xxvii.

21. Review from *Ya* quoted in Álvaro, p. 111.

22. "Autocrítica," p. 126.

23. The homosexual relationship is not explicitly mentioned in the play, but the inference is clear.

24. Holt, p. 104.

25. Fernando Castán Palomar, review reprinted in *Teatro español, 1958-1959*, p. 129.

26. Álvaro, *El espectador y la crítica: El teatro en España en 1965* (Valladolid: Edición del autor, 1966), pp. 340-41, 372.

27. Ruiz Iriarte, "Nota del autor" to *El carrusell*, ed. Marion P. Holt (New York: Appleton-Century-Crofts, 1970), p. xix.

28. *El carrusell* in *Teatro selecto*, p. 306. References are to this edition and are cited in the text as *CA*.

29. Holt, *The Contemporary Spanish Theater*, p. 105.

30. *Ibid.*, p. 104.

31. *Ibid.*; Molero Manglano, pp. 178-83.

32. John E. Dial noted the "Pirandellian overtones" in his review of the Holt edition of *El carrusell*. See *Hispania*, 54 (1971), 614.

33. Marqueríe, review in *Pueblo* quoted by Álvaro, *El espectador y la crítica: El teatro en España en 1964* (Valladolid: Edición del autor, 1965), p. 170; Holt, p. 105.

34. Jacques Guicharnaud, *Modern French Theatre from Giraudoux to Genet* (New Haven & London: Yale University Press, 1967), p. 132.

35. Alba della Fazia, *Jean Anouilh* (New York: Twayne, 1969), p. 17.

36. *Ibid.*, p. 86.

37. The word *comedia* in Spanish has a more general use than "comedy" and may apply to any play.

38. Álvaro, *El espectador y la crítica: El teatro en España en 1967* (Valladolid: Edición del autor, 1965), p. 125.

39. Holt, p. 108.

40. Review from *Marca* quoted by Álvaro, p. 126.

41. González Ruiz, review reprinted in *Teatro español, 1967-1968* (Madrid: Aguilar, 1969), p. 90.

42. *La señora recibe una carta* (Madrid: Alfil, 1967), pp. 25-26.

43. Álvaro, *El espectador y la crítica: El teatro en España en 1969* (Valladolid: Edición del autor, 1970), p. 21.

44. Holt, pp. 108-09.

45. *Historia de un adulterio* (Madrid: Escelicer, 1969), p. 37. References are to this edition and are cited in the text as *S*.

46. See, for example, Marqueríe review quoted by Álvaro, p. 25; López Sancho review, reprinted in *Teatro español, 1968-1969* (Madrid: Aguilar, 1970), p. 301.

47. Marqueríe, *op. cit.*

48. López Sancho, *op. cit.*, p. 300.

Chapter Seven

1. Holt and Woodyard, "Introduction" to Ruiz Iriarte, *Tres telecomedias de España* (Lexington, Mass.: D. C. Heath, 1971), p. ix. The information which follows in this paragraph is from this same source.

2. Ruiz Iriarte, "Prólogo" to *La pequeña comedia* (Madrid: Escelicer, 1967), pp. 10-11. References are to this edition and are cited in the text as *L*.

Chapter Eight

1. In 1960 the exchange rate was approximately 60 *pesetas* to an American dollar. The "fortune" Mateo finds was thus worth less than $17,000.

2. See the review of *De París viene mamá* in Álvaro, *El espectador y la crítica: El teatro en España en 1960* (Valladolid: Edición del Autor, 1961), pp. 94-96.

3. Ruiz Iriarte, "Autocrítica" to *La muchacha del sombrerito rosa* (Madrid: Alfil, 1967), p. 5. References are to this edition and are cited in the text as *M*.

4.   Sainz de Robles, *Teatro español, 1966-67* (Madrid: Aguilar, 1968), p. xvi.

5.   Sainz de Robles erroneously refers to Esteban's second marriage (*Ibid*, p. xv). S. Samuel Trifilo is even more in error when he states that Esteban's second wife was an Argentine girl and that Leonor did not remarry because of her love for Esteban. [See "The Madrid Theater: 1967-68," *Hispania* 52 (1969), 913.] Esteban's lover, as we shall note later, was Spanish, and Leonor, of course, could not "remarry" even if she no longer loved Esteban in that they had never divorced.

6.   For a brief commentary on the subject, see my "Feminine Roles and Attitudes toward Marriage in the Comedies of Miguel Mihura," *Romance Notes* 14 (1973), 445-49. In López Rubio's *La venda en los ojos* (1954), for example, Beatriz goes mad or at least feigns madness when her husband leaves her.

7.   Jaime Salom in his recent play *La piel del limón* (1976) deals with the need for divorce reform in Spain and does show to some extent the psychological problems of the man, his wife, and "the other woman." Ruiz Iriarte's sensitive development of the situation in *La muchacha del sombrerito rosa* is perhaps more analogous, however, to certain novelistic treatments of legal separation and divorce in Spain such as Elena Quiroga's *Algo pasa en la calle* (1954), and Mercedes Salisachs' *La última aventura* (1967) or *Adagio confidencial* (1973), particularly given his apparent understanding of the two women's points of view.

8.   Although Leonor is a strong, admirable, and, in some ways, liberated woman, her ideas are clearly not those of a women's rightist. Marita says she plans to study medicine in Germany, Paloma intends to study architecture in Switzerland, and Belén wants to go to Russia to study ballet. Leonor decides that all three will stay in Madrid, study philosophy and letters because it's "very feminine," and marry young (*M*, 71). Obviously her attitude here is very consistent with her portrayal as a whole.

9.   Holt, *The Contemporary Spanish Theater*, p. 109.

10.   One recalls how quickly Casona fell out of favor with the liberal critics after his return to Spain and how his following, ironically, was from the supposedly conservative middle class.

11.   Ruiz Iriarte, *Primavera en la plaza de París* (Madrid: Alfil, 1968), p. 67. References are to this edition and are cited in the text as *SP*.

12.   Review from *Ya* quoted by Álvaro, *El espectador y la crítica: El teatro en España en 1968* (Valladolid: Edición del Autor, 1969), pp. 13-14.

13.   I am indebted to the author for allowing me to use a manuscript version of the play. In that *Buenas noches, Sabina* is not yet available in its final published form, I am not attempting a detailed analysis of the comedy at this time.

14.   Adolfo Prego, review in *ABC*, September 27, 1975, p. 49.

15.   Review from *Ya* quoted in Álvaro, *El espectador y la crítica: El teatro en España en 1975* (Madrid: Prensa Española, 1976), p. 30.

16. Review from *La Actualidad Española* quoted in Álvaro, *El especta-dor y la crítica: El teatro en España en 1975*, p. 28.
17. Prego.
18. Álvaro, *El espectador y la crítica: El teatro en España en 1975*, p. 31.

Chapter Nine

1. Dowling, pp. 901,902.
2. Dowling, p. 903.
3. *Ibid.*
4. See, for example, Marquerie's review of *Tengo un millón*, *ABC*, February 11, 1960, p. 63. The same observation might, of course, be made of comedies by other Spanish playwrights. Casona is a good case in point.
5. The possible influence of Ruiz Iriarte on other playwrights is a subject of potential interest but lies beyond the scope of the present study. Holt, for example, notes a parallel between *Historia de un adulterio* (1969) and Pemán's *Tres testigos* (1970) (p. 90). There are also obvious ties between Ruiz Iriarte's early plays and some of the comedies of López Rubio in particular. The two authors are friends and may well have discussed their work with each other. Among younger playwrights, both Jaime Salom and Ana Diosdado show occasional points of contact with Ruiz Iriarte's theater. Salom includes Ruiz Iriarte and his poetic theater on a list of Spanish playwrights he admires ["Encuesta," *Primer Acto* 29-30 (December, 1961-January, 1962), 14]. Diosdado, whose father directed four of Ruiz Iriarte's plays in the 1960s, appeared in the cast of *Historia de un adulterio*, a play with which her *Los comuneros* has some structural resemblances. Certain comedies of Santiago Moncada, such as *Salvar a los delfines* (1979), bear strong thematic and technical resemblances to earlier Ruiz Iriarte comedies.
6. Francisco Álvaro lists these works staged outside Spain in his *El espectador y la crítica: El teatro en España en 1969*.

Selected Bibliography

PRIMARY SOURCES

1. Original stage plays (in order of performance. All premières were in
    Madrid unless otherwise indicated. Editions of plays are listed chronolo-
    gically following the data on performances and translations.)

Un día en la gloria (un acto). Zaragoza, 1943; Madrid, 1944.
> Translated into Italian.
> In *Tres comedias optimistas* (Madrid: Artegrafía, 1947);
> With *El aprendiz de amante* (Madrid: Alfil, 1952);
> Excerpt in José Gordon, ed., *Teatro experimental español (Antología e
> historia)* (Madrid: Escelicer, 1965), pp. 115-20.
El puente de los suicidas. San Sebastián, 1944; Madrid, 1945.
> (Madrid: Gráficas Uguina, 1943);
> In *Tres comedias optimistas* (Madrid: Artegrafía, 1947).
Don Juan se ha puesto triste. San Sebastián, 1945; Madrid; 1945.
> Unpublished.
Academia de amor. San Sebastián, 1946; Madrid, 1946.
> In *Tres comedias optimistas* (Madrid: Artegrafía, 1947).
El cielo está cerca. 1947. Unpublished.
La señora, sus ángeles y el diablo. 1947. Unpublished.
El aprendiz de amante. Valencia, 1947; Madrid, 1949. Translated to Portu-
    guese.
> (Madrid: Prensa Castellana, 1949);
> With *Un día en la gloria* (Madrid: Alfil, 1952);
> Excerpts in Antonio Espina, ed., *Las mejores escenas del teatro español
> e hispanoamericano (Desde sus orígenes hasta la época actual)* (Madrid :
> Aguilar, 1959), pp. 1022-27.
Los pájaros ciegos. 1948. Unpublished.
Juanita va a Rio de Janeiro (un acto). 1948.
> In *Colección Teatro (Extra),* No. 100 (Madrid: Alfil, 1954), pp. 139-48.
Las mujeres decentes. Barcelona, 1949; Madrid, 1949. Translated to Portu-
    guese.
> With *El gran minué* (Madrid: Alfil, 1951).
El landó de seis caballos. 1950: Translated into Dutch, English, Portuguese,
    and Japanese.
> (Madrid: Gráficas Cinema, 1950);
> In Sainz de Robles, ed., *Teatro español, 1949-1950* (Madrid: Aguilar,
> 1951);

With *El pobrecito embustero* (Madrid: Alfil, 1953);
In *Teatro selecto de Víctor Ruiz Iriarte* (Madrid: Escelicer, 1967);
Excerpt in Aurelio Labajo, *et al*, eds., *El teatro de 1950*, Vol. I (Madrid: Coculsa, 1970), pp. 23-37.
(Salamanca: Almar, 1979).
El gran minué. 1950.
With *Las mujeres decentes* (Madrid: Alfil, 1951);
(Madrid: Gráficas Cinema, 1951);
In Sainz de Robles, ed., *Teatro español, 1950-1951* (Madrid: Aguilar, 1952);
In *Teatro selecto de Víctor Ruiz Iriarte* (Madrid: Escelicer, 1967).
Cuando ella es la otra. Barcelona: 1951; Madrid: 1952.
Translated into Portuguese.
(Madrid: Alfil, 1952).
Juego de niños. 1952. Translated into German and Portuguese. (Madrid: Alfil, 1951).
In Sainz de Robles, ed., *Teatro español, 1951-1952* (Madrid: Aguilar, 1953).
Excerpt in Fernando Díaz-Plaja, ed., *Teatro español de hoy.*
Antología (1939-1958) (Madrid: Alfil, 1958), pp. 261-76.
Ed. Isabel Magaña Schevill (Englewood Cliffs, N.J.: Prentice-Hall, 1965).
La soltera rebelde. 1952. Translated into Portuguese. (Madrid: Alfil, 1952).
El pobrecito embustero. 1953. Translated into Portuguese.
With *El landó de seis caballos* (Madrid: Alfil, 1953);
In *Teatro*, No. 7 (May, 1953), pp. 49-62;
In Sainz de Robles, ed., *Teatro español, 1952-1953* (Madrid: Aguilar, 1954).
El café de las flores. 1953.
(Madrid: Alfil, 1953).
La cena de los tres reyes. 1954. (Madrid: Alfil, 1955).
Usted no es peligrosa. 1954. (Madrid: Alfil, 1955).
La guerra empieza en Cuba. 1955. Translated into English.
(Madrid: Alfil, 1956);
In Sainz de Robles, ed., *Teatro español, 1955-1956* (Madrid: Aguilar, 1957).
La vida privada de mamá. 1956. Translated into Portuguese. (Madrid: Alfil, 1956).
También la buena gente. Barcelona: 1957. Unpublished.
Esta noche es la víspera. 1958.
(Madrid: Alfil, 1959);
In Sainz de Robles, ed., *Teatro español, 1958-1959.* (Madrid: Aguilar, 1960);
In *Teatro selecto de Víctor Ruiz Iriarte* (Madrid: Escelicer, 1967);
Ed. Judith Merrill. (New York: Odyssey, 1968).
Una investigación privada. 1958. Unpublished.

Tengo un millón. 1960.
    (Madrid: Alfil, 1961).
De París viene mamá. 1960. Unpublished.
El carrusell. 1964.
    (Madrid: Alfil, 1965);
    In Sainz de Robles, ed., *Teatro español, 1964-1965* (Madrid: Aguilar,
    1966);
    In *Teatro selecto de Víctor Ruiz Iriarte* (Madrid: Escelicer, 1967);
    Ed. Marion P. Holt (New York: Appleton-Century-Crofts, 1970).
Un paraguas bajo la lluvia. 1965.
    (Madrid: Alfil, 1966);
    In Sainz de Robles, ed., *Teatro español, 1965-1966* (Madrid: Aguilar,
    1967).
    In *Teatro selecto de Víctor Ruiz Iriarte* (Madrid: Escelicer, 1967).
La muchacha del sombrerito rosa. 1967.
    (Madrid: Alfil, 1967);
    In Sainz de Robles, ed., *Teatro español, 1966-1967* (Madrid: Aguilar,
    1968).
La señora recibe una carta. 1967.
    (Madrid: Alfil, 1967);
    In Sainz de Robles, ed., *Teatro español, 1967-1968* (Madrid: Aguilar,
    1969).
Primavera en la plaza de París. 1968.
    (Madrid: Alfil, 1968).
Historia de un adulterio. 1969.
    (Madrid: Escelicer, 1969);
    In Sainz de Robles, ed., *Teatro español, 1968-1969* (Madrid: Aguilar,
    1970).
Buenas noches, Sabina. 1975. Unpublished.

2.   Other published dramatic works

RATTIGAN, TERENCE. *El príncipe durmiente.* Trans. Diego Hurtado. Adapted
    by Víctor Ruiz Iriarte. Madrid: Alfil, 1958.
SHAKESPEARE, WILLIAM. *La fierecilla domada.* Versión libre de Víctor Ruiz
    Iriarte. Madrid: Alfil, 1959.
La pequeña comedia. Madrid: Escelicer, 1967. Contains the following televi-
    sion plays: *Milady, objectos para regalo; El presidente y la felicidad; Un
    revuelo de palomas; Un ramo de rosas; Cándida; Amador, el optimista;
    El collar; El secreto; Sala de espera; El buscador de maravillas; La fuga;
    El piso; El café.*
Tres telecomedias de España. Eds. Marion P. Holt and George W.
    Woodyard. Lexington, Mass.: D.C. Heath, 1971. Contains *Amador, el
    optimista; El presidente y la felicidad; Sala de espera.*

3. Selected essays

"Prólogo" to *Tres comedias optimistas.* Madrid: Artegrafía, 1947. Pp. 3-6. Ruiz Iriarte's early defense of a poetic theater.

"Viaje alrededor de un escenario." Four-part memoirs published in *Teatro*: 1 (Nov., 1952), 41-45; 2 (Dec., 1952), 42-47; 3 (Jan., 1953), 37-41; 6 (April, 1953), 25-30. Single best source of information on author's childhood and early career. Also important for his perception of the changes in the Madrid literary world from the 1930s to the postwar period.

"Alfonso Paso." *Primer Acto* 3 (Summer, 1957), 21-22. Generous praise for the younger playwright as well as several general observations on theater.

Un pequeño mundo. Madrid: S.G.A. E., 1962. Includes a prologue by the author and a selection of twenty-eight of his numerous newspaper articles.

Tres maestros (Arniches, Benavente y Valle-Inclán). Madrid: Real Escuela Superior de Arte Dramático, 1965. 30 pp. Lecture presented at official opening of the dramatic arts school for academic year 1965-66. Important for Ruiz Iriarte's own view of theater and theatrical vocation.

"Prólogo" to Francisco Álvaro, *El espectador y la crítica: El teatro en España en 1966.* Valladolid: Edición del Autor, 1967. Pp. ix-xiv. Interesting observations on contemporary theater.

"Prólogo" to *La pequeña comedia.* Madrid: Escelicer, 1967. Pp. 9-13. Defense of television plays as valid literary genre.

"Prólogo" to *Teatro selecto de Víctor Ruiz Iriarte.* Madrid: Escelicer, 1967. Pp. 5-12. Some informative comments on the five plays chosen for the anthology and on his view of theater.

"Prólogo" to *Teatro selecto de Edgar Neville.* Madrid: Escelicer, 1968. Pp. 5-11. Favorable portrait of a fellow playwright. Evokes the Madrid of Neville's youth as well as his character and characteristics.

SECONDARY SOURCES

The single best source for reviews of Ruiz Iriarte's plays is the yearly anthology *Teatro español*, edited by Federico Carlos Sainz de Robles and published in Madrid by Aguilar. Works by Ruiz Iriarte appear in the volumes for 1949-50, 1950-51, 1951-52, 1952-53, 1955-56, 1958-59, 1964-65, 1965-66, 1966-67, 1967-68, 1968-69. Each play is accompanied by the author's self-criticism along with selected critical reaction.

ÁLVARO, FRANCISCO. *El espectador y la crítica.* Valladolid: Edición del autor, annual publication. This yearbook provides a synthesis of critical reaction to selected plays. Volumes including sections dedicated to individual works by Ruiz Iriarte are those for 1958, 1960, 1964, 1965, 1967, 1968, 1969, and 1975.

ARAGONÉS, JUAN EMILIO. *Teatro español de posguerra*. Madrid: Publicaciones Españolas, 1971. Pp. 57-62. Good introduction to Ruiz Iriarte's theater. Emphasizes the comedies of customs and the *pobrecito* character.

BAQUERO GOYANES, ARCADIO. "El humor en el teatro de Ruiz Iriarte" in *El teatro de humor en España* by J. Rof Carballo *et al*. Madrid: Editora Nacional, 1966. Pp. 187-99. Primarily a discussion of the *pobrecito* as a key character in five of Ruiz Iriarte's comedies. Also includes an interview with the playwright.

BORING, PHYLLIS ZATLIN. "The Bases of Humor in the Contemporary Spanish Theater." Ph.D. dissertation, University of Florida, 1965. Extensive discussion of comic techniques and situations. Includes references to nine of Ruiz Iriarte's plays from the 1950s. Relevant excerpts have appeared in *Kentucky Foreign Language Quarterly*, Supplement 13 (1967), 41-51; and *Romance Notes*, 11 (1969), 8-11.

_____. Introduction to *El landó de seis caballos*. Salamanca: Almar, 1979. Pp. 11-25. Discussion of Ruiz Iriarte's theater in general and his place in Spanish theater. In Spanish.

_____. "The Pirandellism of Víctor Ruiz Iriarte." *Estreno* 4 ii (Fall, 1978), 18-21. Discussion of six plays, three from among the early comedies of poetic fantasy and three from among the serious plays of the 1960s. Concludes that *Historia de un adulterio* is the most Pirandellist of Ruiz Iriarte's works.

GIULIANO, WILLIAM. *Buero Vallejo, Sastre y el teatro de su tiempo*. New York: Las Américas, 1971. Pp. 39-46. Discusses eight plays by Ruiz Iriarte, giving brief synopsis and critical reaction. Generally negative criticism.

HOLT, MARION P. Introduction to *El carrusell*. New York: Appleton-Century-Crofts, 1970. Pp. xi-xvii. Brief but excellent introduction to subject. Written in Spanish.

_____. "Victor Ruiz Iriarte." In *The Contemporary Spanish Theater (1949-1972)*. Boston: Twayne, 1975. Pp. 98-109. More extensive analysis of Ruiz Iriarte's theater, with emphasis on later, more serious works. Highly recommended.

LENDÍNEZ-GALLEGO, ESTEBAN. *El teatro de Ruiz Iriarte*. Madrid: Ediciones Cultura Hispanica, 1973. Prologue by Lorenzo López Sancho. A rather disappointing study of only fifteen plays. Marred by superficial analyses of individual works and a fragmentary style, but does, however, identify certain recurring themes in Ruiz Iriarte's theater. Particular emphasis on *El carrusell*.

MARQUERÍE, ALFREDO. *Veinte años de teatro en España*. Madrid: Editora Nacional, 1959. Pp. 167-76. Important as early study frequently cited by other critics. Brief comments on individual plays, including three of the unpublished ones. Marred by some dubious comparisons with other playwrights and by some misinterpretations of plays.

MOLERO MANGLANO, LUIS. *Teatro español contemporáneo*. Madrid: Editora

Nacional, 1974. Pp. 170-83. Previously appeared in English under title "Meanings and Motives in Spanish Theatre," *Spain Today*, 12 (April, 1971), 41-46. Attempts to identify the dominant characteristics of Ruiz Iriarte's theater across the years. Interesting comparison of *Juego de niños* and *El carrusell*.

MORALES, MARÍA VICTORIA. "The Farcical Mode in the Spanish Theater of the Twentieth Century." Ph.D. dissertation, Columbia University, 1969. Extensive discussion of comic techniques and situations. Includes references to nine of Ruiz Iriarte's comedies, primarily from the 1950s.

O'CONNOR, PATRICIA W. "Víctor Ruiz Iriarte habla de la comedia española." *Estreno* 4ii (Fall, 1978), 16-17. Recent interview with helpful insights into playwright's view of current state of Spanish theater.

ORTA, DOMINGO. "Gente de teatro en España (I): Víctor Ruiz Iriarte." *Teatro*, 17 (Sept.-Dec., 1955), 29-32, 76-77. Interesting interview in which the playwright discusses his views on theater in general and on some aspects of his own work.

PÉREZ MINIK, DOMINGO. *Teatro europeo contemporáneo*. Madrid: Guadarrama, 1961. Pp. 449-61. Very interesting analysis of Ruiz Iriarte's theater in general and its relationship to Spanish escapist comedy.

RODRÍGUEZ, RICHART J. "Entre renovacion y tradicíon. Direcciones principales del teatro español actual," *Boletín de la Biblioteca de Menéndez Pelayo*, 41 (1965), 383-418. Very brief, negative commentary on Ruiz Iriarte, but important for its lucid explanation of the literary value of the so-called escapist theater.

RUIZ RAMÓN, FRANCISCO. *Historia del teatro español, 2: Siglo XX*. Madrid: Alianza, 1971. Pp. 355-56. Rapid review of the major critical opinions on Ruiz Iriarte's theater.

SCHEVILL, ISABEL MAGAÑA. Introduction to *Juego de niños*. Englewood Cliffs, N.J.: Prentice-Hall, 1965. Pp. viii-xxiii. Interesting introduction to Ruiz Iriarte's theater, particularly important for its identification of the recurring use of an "authentic" individual within a dramatic formula. Finds a tragic undercurrent even in his comedies and farces. Some slight errors in interpretations of individual plays. Recommended.

TORRENTE BALLESTER, GONZALO. *Teatro español contemporáneo*. 2nd ed. Madrid: Guadarrama, 1968. Pp. 579-88. Reviews of eight plays from the 1950s. Balanced criticism.

TRENAS, JULIO. "Víctor Ruiz Iriarte, Presidente de la S.G.A.E.," *ABC*, July 22, 1969, n.p. Informative interview in which Ruiz Iriarte mentions the highlights of his professional career.

VALBUENA PRAT, ÁNGEL. *Historia del teatro español*. Barcelona: Noguer, 1956. Pp. 665-71. Generally positive look at several of the playwright's more important early works.

WADE, GERALD E. "The Comedies of Víctor Ruiz Iriarte." *Hispania* 45 (1962), 704-11. Emphasis on function of comedy in general. Superficial, somewhat negative commentary on several of Ruiz Iriarte's plays.

Index

(The works of Ruiz Iriarte are listed under his name)

ABC (newspaper), 21

Achard, Marcel, 130n27

Alarcón, Pedro Antonio de, *El capitán Veneno* (Captain Poison), 20

Alonso, José Luis, 19, 84

Alvarez Quintero, Serafín and Joaquín, *Mañana de sol* (Sunny morning), 104

Alvaro, Francisco, 96, 97, 123

Anouilh, Jean, 24, 27, 39, 44, 48–49, 75, 93–94, 125, 130n27; *Alouette, L'* (The lark), 20; *Ardèle ou la Marguerite*, 94; *Bal des voleurs, Le* (The thieves' ball), 48; *Cher Antoine ou l'amour raté* (Dear Antoine or the love that failed), 86; *Invitation au chateau, L'* (Invitation to the chateau), 48–49, 76; *Léocadia*, 39–40; *Valse des toréadors, La* (The toreadors' waltz), 48

Arias, María, 17

Arniches, Carlos, 14, 53, 68, 132n5; *Es mi hombre*, 132n5; *señor Badanas, El*, 132n5; *sobrina de cura, La* (The priest's niece), 13–14

Arout, Gabriel, *Manzanas para Eva* (Apples for Eve), 20

Azorín, 30

Baquero Goyanes, Arcadio, 36, 53, 54, 61, 64

Bekeffi, Istuan, *Mi noche de bodas* (My wedding night), 19

Benavente, Jacinto, 14, 22, 23, 52, 75, 121, 133n22; *cursi, Lo*, 133n22; *intereses creados, Los* (The bonds of interest), 47, 49

boulevard comedies, 56, 68, 73, 74; *See also* vaudeville

Buero Vallejo, Antonio, 26, 102; *Historia de una escalera* (Story of a stairway), 24

Calderón de la Barca, Pedro, 34

Calvo-Sotelo, Joaquín, 26; *María Antonieta* (Marie Antoinette), 38; *muralla, La* (The wall); 98–99

Campoamor, Ramón de, 104

Carbonell, Carmen, 18, 19, 54, 61, 68, 133n37

Casaravilla, Carlos, 66

Casero, Antonio, 14

Casona, Alejandro, 18, 22, 23, 27, 29–33, 35, 44, 116, 129n6, 129n13, 138n10; *árboles mueren de pie, Los* (Trees die standing), 30, 31, 32–33, 41; *Prohibido suicidarse en primavera* (Suicide prohibited in the spring), 27, 29, 31–32, 41; *Siete gritos en el mar*, 136n16; *sirena varada, La* (The stranded mermaid), 29, 30–31, 41; *tres perfectas casadas, Las* (The three perfect wives), 96, 97

Castro, Guillén de, *Las mocedades del Cid* (The young Cid), 116

Cela, Camilo José, 16; *La familia de Pascual Duarte* (The family of Pascual Duarte), 16

censorship, 22, 23, 82, 94

Cervantes, Miguel de, 34, 53; *Don Quixote*, 132n5

Chaplin, Charlie, 13

Christie, Agatha, 87; *The Mousetrap*, 87

Ciudad (newspaper), 15

comedy of manners, 18, 19, 20, 23, 25, 43, 45, 52–74, 75, 84, 110, 113, 116, 122, 125

Coward, Noel, 24; *Blithe Spirit*, 135n13

Cuesta, Miguel de la, *Dos mujeres a las nueve*, 133n22

della Fazia, Alba, 94

detective comedies, 87, 113–15

Diosdado, Ana, 139n5; *Los comuneros*, 139n5
Diosdado, Enrique, 21, 89, 97, 115, 119, 133n37
Don Juan, 18, 20, 45, 46, 53, 54–55, 56, 96, 111, 131n6, 132n4
Dowling, John, 124, 128n26
drama, 18, 19, 20, 21, 25, 26, 38, 76, 83–101, 108, 110, 125

Echegaray, José, *O locura o santidad* (Madman or saint), 99
Entrambasaguas, Joaquín de, 61
escapist theater, 24, 36, 38, 44, 52, 54, 74, 94, 126
Español, El (magazine), 16
Espina, Concha, 15
Estafeta Literaria, La (magazine), 16
evasionist theater. *See* escapist theater
Evreinov, Nikolai, 18, 27, 30–32, 34, 39, 44, 125, 129n6; *The Main Thing*, 30–32, 34, 43
existentialism, 100–101

Fantasía (magazine), 16
farce, 19, 20, 23, 26, 29, 40, 45–51, 52, 54–63, 65, 68, 70, 74, 75–82, 83, 89, 90, 93, 94, 110, 120, 125; farcical, 106, 114, 118
Fernández Cuenca, Carlos, 68
flashback technique, 85, 86, 90, 93, 97, 98, 99, 100

Galdós. *See* Pérez Galdós
Garcés, Isabel, 71
García Álvarez, Enrique, 14
García Lorca, Federico, 22, 25; *La zapatera prodigiosa* (The shoemaker's prodigious wife), 62–63
Garcilaso (magazine), 16
Gascó, Tina, 17, 18, 19, 28, 41, 63, 66, 73, 76, 133n37
Giraudoux, Jean, 24, 48; *Electre*, 48; *Guerre de Troie n'aura pas lieu, La* (The Trojan War will not take place), 48
González Ruiz, Nicolás, 97
Granada, Fernando, 17
Guerrero, María, 13

Hartnoll, Phyllis, 24
historical settings, 18, 19, 50, 76, 80, 131n15
Hitler, Adolf, 15
Holt, Marion P., 19, 39, 47, 49, 68, 83, 85, 92, 96–97, 102, 119

Informaciones (newspaper), 20
Iriarte Sanz, Emilia (mother), 13, 14, 17

Jardiel Poncela, Enrique, 22; *marido de ida y vuelta, Un*, 135n13; *sexo débil ha hecho gimnasia, El* (The weaker sex has undergone gymnastics), 81

Lendínez-Gallego, Esteban, 83, 131n6
Lerroux, Alejandro, 15
López Rubio, José, 19, 23, 25, 45, 53, 102, 128n27, 139n5; *Alberto*, 59; *Diana está comunicando*, 133n22; *otra orilla, La* (The other shore), 108; *venda en los ojos, La* (The blindfold), 38, 138n6
López Sancho, Lorenzo, 53–54, 100
Luca de Tena, Cayetano, 19
Luca de Tena, Juan Ignacio, *Dos mujeres a las nueve*, 133n22

McKay, Douglas R., 132n17
Mallorquí, José, *Papá, mi caballo y tú* (Papa, my horse and you), 20; *secreto de Tomy, El* (Tomy's secret), 20
Marivaux, Pierre de Chamblain de, 25
Marqueríe, Alfredo, 36, 50, 83, 131n6
Marsillach, Adolfo, 114
Merrill, Judith S., 85
middle class: as audience, 22, 24, 54, 94, 97, 123; as subject, 74, 90, 93, 94, 103, 107, 111, 117, 119, 125, 126
Mihura, Miguel, 19, 23, 87, 102, 132n17; *Tres sombreros de copa* (Three top hats), 107, 133n22
Miller, Arthur, *Death of a Salesman*, 90; *View from the Bridge, A*, 90
Mix, Tom, 13
Molero Manglano, Luis, 53, 84, 92, 131n15
Molière, 75
Moncada, Salvador, *Salvar a los delfines*, 139n5

Monleón, José, 24
Morales, María Victoria, 58
Mourlane Michelena, Pedro, 15
Mullor, Enrique, 16

Neville, Edgar, 23, 25, 45, 53
Noticiero Universal, El (newspaper), 20

Parada de la Puente, Manuel, 20
Paso, Alfonso, 87, 128n27, 136n16; *bomba llamada Abelardo, Una* (A bomb named Abelard), 50; *Cena de matrimonios* (Dinner for married couples), 96; *Juicio contra un sinvergüenza* (Judgment against a ne'er-do-well), 96
Pemán, José María, 22; *Tres testigos*, 139n5
Pennella, Emma, 76
Pérez Galdós, Benito, 13, 53; *Fortunata y Jacinta*, 132n5
Pérez Minik, Domingo, 25, 45, 53, 73
Pirandello, Luigi, 18, 24, 27, 30, *34–35*, 44, 93, 125, 129n13; *As Well As Before, Better Than Before*, 35; *Henry IV*, 38–39, 40; *It Is So (If You Think So)*, 35; *Six Characters in Search of an Author*, 99; Pirandellian, 35, 39, 58, 92–93, 96, 97, 99, 100
Plautus, 76
pobrecita, 58, 70, 71, *129–30n17*, 132n4
pobrecito, 36, 40, 43, 48, 51, 53, 54, 61, 62, 64, 66, 67, 69, 74, 87, 88, 110, 111, 114, 122, 125, 129–30n17, 132n4, 132n5
poetic fantasy, 18, 19, 23, 25, *27–44*, 52, 54, 55, 59, 68, 75, 103, 107, 108, 112, 125
Prego, Adolfo, 122
Priestley, J. B., 86–87; *Dangerous Corner*, 86, 96; *I Have Been Here Before*, 86; *Inspector Calls, An*, 93, 96

Quevedo, Francisco, 45
Quiroga, Elena, *Algo pasa en la calle*, 138n7

Rattigan, Terence, *The Sleeping Prince*, 20
Rodríguez, Victoria, 66
Rodríguez de León, A., 68

Rodríguez Richart, J., 23, 25
Roussin, André, 68, 134n44; *Nina*, 20
Ruiz Fraguas, Víctor (father), 13, 14, 17
Ruiz Iriarte, María Francisca (sister), 13, 14, 17
Ruiz Iriarte, María Luisa (sister), 13, 14, 17
Ruiz Iriarte, Pilar (sister), 13, 14, 17
Ruiz Iriarte, Víctor, birth, 13; childhood, 13–14; collaboration in literary magazines, 16, 20; director, 17, 19, 21, 80, 121; early discouragement, 15, 127n5; education, 14; essays, 20, 21–22, 61; fame outside Spain, 19, 26, 63, 126, 128n27; first commercial success, 18, 54; first efforts at writing plays, 14; first play staged, 16; *"Juventud Creadora"* (postwar literary group), 16; Madrid as background to plays, 33, 50, 110; María Rolland Prize, 21, 119; motion pictures, 17, 19–20, 63, 76, 102–103; National Literature Prize, 21, 116; National Television Prize, 21, 102; National Theater Prize, 19, 63; newspaper career, 15–16, 20, 21, 61; opinion of tragicomedy, 68; period of great productivity, 19, 66; Piquer Prize, 18, 33; play adaptations, 20; preference for comedy, 25–26, 75, 83, 95, 124; president of association of Spanish writers, 21; president of writers' pension fund, 21; private life, 17; residence in Madrid, 13, 17; television, 17, 19–20, 21, *102–12*; travels, 17; views on theater, 14–15, 16, 22–23, 25–26, 27, 75, 125; witness to changing Spanish society, 20, 21–22, 49, 52, 54, 58, 60–61, 71, 73–74, 83–84, 89, 92, 94, 95, 97, 99, 100, 103–104, 111, 116–17, *125–26*

WORKS:
Academia de amor. See *Academy of Love*
Academy of Love, 18, 27, *33–36*, 40, 42, 43, 44, 57, 59, 84, 130n18
Amador, el optimista. See *Amador, the Optimist*
Amador, the Optimist, 107, 110, 111, 114
Apartment, The, 110

Apprentice Lover, The, 18, 19, 52, 53, 54–58, 59, 60, 61, 69, 72, 106

aprendiz de amante, El. *See The Apprentice Lover*

Blind Birds, 18, 83

Bouquet of Roses, A, 106, 110

Buenas noches, Sabina. *See Good Evening, Sabina*

buscador de maravillas, El. *See The Seeker of Miracles*

café, El. *See The Cafe*

Cafe, The, 105

café de las flores, El. *See The Flowers Cafe*

Cándida, 105–106

Carousel, The, 20, 76, 83, 84, 89–94, 95, 97, 98, 108, 109, 111, 113, 115, 126

carrusell, El. *See The Carousel*

cena de los tres reyes, La. *See The Dinner of the Three Kings*

Child's Play, 19, 52, 53, 54, 63–66, 67, 68, 74, 84, 92, 96, 123

cielo está cerca, El. *See Heaven Is Near*

collar, El. *See The Necklace*

Cuando ella es la otra. *See When She Is the Other Woman*

Day in Glory, A, 16–17, 28, 45–46, 51, 71

De París viene mamá. *See Mama's Coming from Paris*

día en la gloria, Un. *See A Day in Glory*

Dinner of the Three Kings, The, 45, 50–51

Don Juan Has Become Sad, 18

Don Juan se ha puesto triste. *See Don Juan Has Become Sad*

Elena, I Love You, 20

Elena, te quiero. *See Elena, I Love You*

Esta noche es la víspera. *See Tonight Is the Prelude*

Flight, The, 109–10

Flock of Pigeons, A, 107, 111

Flowers Cafe, The, 27, 41–43, 52, 53, 66, 84, 87, 106, 118

fuga, La. *See The Flight*

Girl in the Little Pink Hat, The, 21, 113, 115–19, 120, 122

Good Evening, Sabina, 21, 113, 121–23

Good People, Too, 19

gran minué, El. *See The Grand Minuet*

Grand Minuet, The, 18, 45, 46–50, 51, 52, 92, 99, 126

guerra empieza en Cuba, La. *See The War Begins in Cuba*

Heaven Is Near, 18

Historia de un adulterio. *See Story of Adultery*

I Have a Million, 113–15, 126

investigación privada, Una. *See A Private Investigation*

Juanita Goes to Rio de Janeiro, 18, 83, 84–85

Juanita va a Rio de Janeiro. *See Juanita Goes to Rio de Janeiro*

Juego de niños. *See Child's Play*

Lady, Her Angels and the Devil, The, 18

Lady Receives a Letter, The, 21, 83, 94–97, 109, 111

landó de seis caballos, El. *See The Six-Horse Landau*

Little Theater, 21, 102–12

Mama's Coming from Paris, 19, 114, 115

"Milady," Gift Shop, 104, 105, 106

"Milady," Objetos para regalos. *See "Milady," Gift Shop*

muchacha del sombrerito rosa, La. *See The Girl in the Little Pink Hat*

mujeres decentes, Las. *See Respectable Women*

Necklace, The, 109, 110

pájaros ciegos, Los. *See Blind Birds*

paraguas bajo la lluvia, Un. *See An Umbrella Under the Rain*

pequeña comedia, La. *See Little Theater*

pequeño mundo, Un. *See A Small World*

piso, El. *See The Apartment*

pobrecito embustero, El. *See The Poor Little Liar*

Poor Little Liar, The, 52, 53, 68–71, 74, 122, 126, 130n3

President and Happiness, The, 108, 110, 111

presidente y la felicidad, El. *See The President and Happiness*

Primavera en la plaza de París. See
   Springtime in the Plaza de París
Private Investigation, A, 19, 87, 114,
   115
Private Life of Mama, The, 72–74, 76,
   115
puente de los suicidas, El. See Suicide
   Bridge
ramo de rosas, Un. See A Bouquet of
   Roses
Rebellious Spinster, The, 52, 53, 66–
   68, 74
Respectable Women, 18, 52, 53, 58–60,
   71
revuelo de palomas, Un. See A Flock of
   Pigeons
Sala de espera. See The Waiting Room
Secret, The, 109, 110, 111
secreto, El. See The Secret
Seeker of Miracles, The, 107
señora recibe una carta, La. See The
   Lady Receives a Letter
señora, sus ángeles y el diablo, La. See
   The Lady, Her Angels and the Devil
Six-Horse Landau, The, 18, 27, 36–41,
   42, 43, 44, 52, 59, 72, 84, 105, 106,
   126
Small World, A, 20
soltera rebelde, La. See The Rebellious
   Spinster
Springtime in the Plaza de París, 21,
   113, 115, 119–21
Story of Adultery, 21, 83, 97–101, 108,
   111, 113, 115, 126, 139n5
Suicide Bridge, 16, 17, 18, 27, 28–33,
   34, 35, 36, 40, 41, 42, 43, 59, 106
También la buena gente. See Good
   People, Too
Tengo un millón. See I Have a Million
Tonight Is the Prelude, 19, 83, 85–89,
   92, 95, 96, 98, 108, 111, 113, 114,
   115, 126
Umbrella Under the Rain, An, 21, 76,
   80–82, 89, 105, 113
Usted no es peligrosa. See You're Not
   Dangerous
vida privada de mamá, La. See The
   Private Life of Mama
Waiting Room, The, 108–109, 111
War Begins in Cuba, The, 19, 75, 76–
   80, 85

When She Is the Other Woman, 53,
   60–63, 64, 72, 74, 122, 123
You're Not Dangerous, 71–72, 73, 74,
   76

Rusiñol, Santiago, 14

sainete (popular farce), 14
Sainz de Robles, Federico Carlos, 26, 68,
   87, 116, 128n26, 134n41
Salisachs, Mercedes, *Adagio confiden-*
   cial, 138n7; *última aventura, La,*
   138n7
Salom, Jaime, 139n5; *La piel del limón,*
   138n7
Sartre, Jean Paul, *Huis clos* (No exit),
   101; Sartrean, 100–101
Sastre, Alfonso, 24
satire, 18, 19, 45–51, 56–57, 58, 70–71,
   94, 103, 107, 108, 109, 111, 117, 120,
   125, 126, 130n3; satirical, 22, 26, 68, 99
Schevill, Isabel Magaña, 29, 37, 52–53,
   54–55, 58, 65, 83, 85
Schneider, Eric, *Las tres gracias de la*
   casa de enfrente (The three graces from
   the house across the street), 20
Scribe, Eugène, 134n10
Serna, Víctor de la, 15
Shakespeare, William, *Comedy of*
   Errors, The, 134n7; *Midsummer*
   Night's Dream, A, 75; *Taming of the*
   Shrew, The, 20
Shaw, George Bernard, 59, 131n6; *Man*
   and Superman, 56
Sol, El (newspaper), 15–16
Soldevilla Durante, Ignacio, 23
Solft, André, *Mi noche de bodas* (My
   wedding night), 19
Sordo, Enrique, 24
Soriano de Andia, Vicente:
   Ayer . . . será mañana (Yester-
   day . . . will be tomorrow), 38, 135n13
Spanish Civil War, 16, 22, 23, 24, 81,
   116, 119–20
Steinbeck, John, *The Wayward Bus,* 86
Suárez de Deza, Enrique, *Una gran*
   señora (A great lady), 19

Torre, Amelia de la, 21, 89, 97, 115, 119,
   133n37

Torrente Ballester, Gonzalo, 51, 61, 65, 66, 71, 76
tragicomedy, 68, 74, 93, 125

Valbuena Prat, Ángel, 29, 44, 52
Valle-Inclán, Ramón, 45, 49
Vaszary, Janos, 20
vaudeville, 25, 26, 68, 72, 83, 94, 125; *See also* boulevard comedies

Vico, Antonio, 18, 19, 54, 61, 68, 133n37
Villaespesa, Francisco, 14

Wade, Gerald E., 47, 67, 73, 131n13, 132n17, 134n10, 136n16
Wilde, Oscar, 24
Woodyard, George W., 102

Zilhay, Lajos, *La puerta abierta* (The open door), 20